10

j641.5   Borghese, Anita
B732i   The international cookie jar cookbook.
           Drawings by Yaroslava Mills. New York,
           Scribner, c1975.
                               7.95   74-14075

                 1.Cooking. I.Title.

5/76

The INTERNATIONAL COOKIE JAR Cookbook

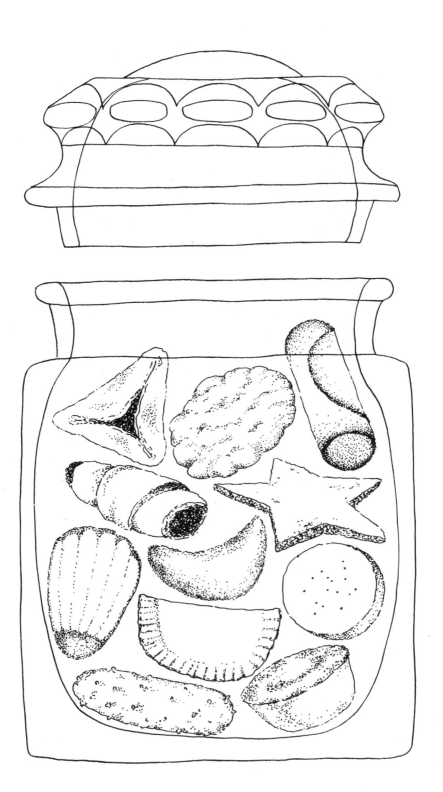

The INTERNATIONAL COOKIE JAR Cookbook

ANITA BORGHESE

DRAWINGS BY YAROSLAVA MILLS

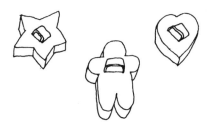

Charles Scribner's Sons · New York ·

Printed in the United States of America
Library of Congress Catalog Card Number 74-14075
ISBN 0-684-144077

Contents

10

Cookies from Africa and the Middle East

Cookies from the Far East, Pacific Islands, and Australia

Cookies from North America and the West Indies

Cookies from Central America and South America

Index

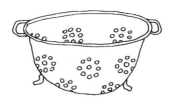

Acknowledgments

Special thanks to Dorothy Johnson of the Mount Pleasant Library, Pleasantville, N. Y., for her help and kind inspiration.

Thanks and appreciation to Jewell Fenzi and Helen Dovale of *This Is the Way We Cook*, for their recipe for *Panlevi* from Curaçao.

For their generous sharing of recipes, grateful thanks to June Taubman, Bennetta Fajardo, Maria Castro, Margaret Parke, Alfredo Salazar, Dina Koegler, Pauline Lafferty, Mrs. Olga Tolstoy and Mrs. Tanya Tolstoy Penkrat, Mrs. A. Trouw of Rijsoord, Holland, and Maria Ramos of La Coruña, Spain.

For their kind cooperation in providing information, thanks to the Arab Information Center, Australian News and Information Bureau, Austrian Information Service, Bulgarian Tourist Office, Congo Brazzaville Mission to the United Nations, Ghana News Agency, Consul General of Iceland, Jamaica Tourist Board, Consul General of Korea, Lebanon Tourist and Information Office, Consul General of Nigeria, Panama Government Tourist Bureau, Consul General of Switzerland, Thailand Mission to the United Nations, Pema Thonden of Tibetan Arts and Crafts, Anne Pellowski of UNICEF, and Vietnam Permanent Observer to the United Nations, all of New York City; and the Embassy of Tunisia, Washington, D. C.

For her untiring help in the test kitchen, special thanks to my mother.

To Andrea

the sweetest cookie of all.

Introduction

One of my earliest and fondest memories is helping my mother to bake cookies. My favorites were sugar cookies that we rolled out and cut into many different shapes and sizes. My sister and I trimmed them with colored sugar decorations, and at holiday time frosted them and sprinkled them with shiny silver balls or cinnamon candies. I was about six years old at the time, and what I didn't know then was that people all over the world make a great variety of cookies and love the making and the eating as much as we do. Every nation has its favorites, and if you arranged all of these international cookies on a huge platter you'd find just about every size, shape, color, texture, and flavor of cookie you could possibly think of.

It's fun to make these cookies to find out what good things other people eat in different parts of the world. Some of the cookies in this book will be familiar to you because the recipes were brought here by people from other countries so long ago that we think of them now as American. Shortbread, for instance, originally came from Scotland. Another cookie nearly everyone knows is the almond cookie that is served in Chinese restaurants.

In other countries cookies aren't always called cookies. In England a cookie is called a *biscuit*. In Spain it's a *galleta*, in France *gâteau sec* ("dry cake"), in Italy *biscotto*, and in Germany *Keks*. In some places the people don't really have cookies as we know them, but they do have sweetmeats, which are a cross between cookies and candy. The American word *cookie* probably came from the Dutch word *koekje,* which means "little cake."

Each cookie was first made in its native land for a particular reason. Some were made to celebrate a holiday, like the *Zimtsterne* made in Germany at Christmas time. Others were created for special occasions, like the Baptismal Cookies of Costa Rica. Still other cookies were created to use ingredients plentiful in the area—like Peanut Cookies in Nigeria or Oatcakes in Ireland.

Cookies made in countries not on the continents of North America, South America, and Europe are often quite different from the kinds we're used to. In the Far East, for instance, wheat is seldom grown, so cookies or pastries are made with rice flour, barley flour, or even beans. Cookies in Middle Eastern countries are more like little pastries than cookies, and are likely to be filled with nuts and honey. Some African cookies are made with cornmeal instead of flour, and sweetmeats in India are often made with chick peas as a flour substitute.

No one knows when the first cookie was made or in what country, because people have been baking small cakes of one kind or another since they first started to build cooking fires and grind grain to make flour or meal. The first cookies were probably like biscuits or hard cakes. In ancient times they were sometimes used as offerings to pagan gods, especially in Northern Europe where little cakes were baked in the forms of people and animals.

I've gathered the recipes for the cookies in this book from nearly seventy nations all over the world. In nearly every case I've chosen a cookie that's typical of the type made in its native land, that isn't too difficult to make (with a few exceptions that I'll tell about under "Cookie-Making Methods"), and that tastes really good to me. Like Will Rogers, who never met a man he didn't like, I've seldom met a cookie I didn't like, so it was difficult for me to choose just one representative cookie from each country. And it was even more difficult to choose a limited number of countries. I'd have liked to include every nation, but since that wasn't possible from the standpoint of space, I've tried to select the nations I feel best represent each area of the world. If I've omitted a land dear to you or a cookie recipe you feel shouldn't have been left out, I hope you'll understand that my biggest regret is that there wasn't room for *every* nation and *every* cookie.

You'll find a few cookie recipes for which you'll need to shop for one or two unusual ingredients. I hope you'll try some of these special recipes because I think you'll find the new taste experiences they'll bring you particularly rewarding. Just shopping for the ingredients can be an adventure in itself. If the flavors of some of these cookies seem strange to you at first, just keep nibbling until the tastes become more familiar, and you'll have added a new flavor to your life and an appreciation of other people and other cultures.

As you make cookies from the recipes in this book you'll probably become more interested in and aware of foods of other nations as I did. It was great fun, for example, making Japanese *Yokan* for the first time. These cookies were so unusual and so good that I asked my family and friends to taste some and try to guess what was in them. Some thought *Yokan* were made of dates or raisins and others said figs, but everyone thought they were delicious. Everyone was amazed to find out that the main ingredient was beans, something none of us had ever before thought of using to make sweets. When. I was experimenting with Scandinavian cookies I used hartshorn salt as a leavening for the first time, and I found the cookies had a crisp, firm texture quite different from cookies made with baking powder or baking soda.

Let's start now on a trip through many lands with all kinds of cookies to guide us. There are even some special cookies from our own United States.

ANITA BORGHESE

Before You Begin to Bake You'll Want to Know These Things

SOME COOKIE-MAKING METHODS

Drop Cookies: After you've mixed the dough scoop it up, a spoonful at a time, and drop it onto a baking sheet. When you put the cookies into the oven they will flatten out themselves as they bake. Most recipes of this kind will tell you to drop by teaspoonfuls, and you can use any ordinary little spoon because the dough doesn't have to be measured exactly. Since drop cookies are the easiest and quickest kind of cookies to make, they're a good idea for your first attempt at cookie baking.

Shaped Cookies: After you've mixed the dough pull off a small piece with your hand and shape it the way that the recipe tells you to. Most of the time you roll each piece between the palms of your hands to form it into a ball. Then you put it on a baking sheet, and if the recipe says so you press it down a little with the palm of your hand to flatten it. Sometimes you shape the cookies by pressing the dough into a pie plate or jar. The dough may then be baked, sautéed, or chilled, and perhaps cut into wedges or other eatable pieces. Some shaped cookies are made with a special thin dough called phyllo (see page 100) that you buy already made. You fill and roll or fold the dough as the recipe directs. Shaped cookies are easy to make.

Roll and Cut Cookies: After you've mixed the dough sprinkle a tablespoon or two of flour (or sugar if the recipe says so) on your pastry board, take the dough out of the bowl, and set it down on the floured board. With your hand wipe some flour all over a rolling pin, then roll the floured rolling pin back and forth in every direction over the dough until the dough is the size or thickness mentioned in the recipe. This is the way the rolled dough should look if it's

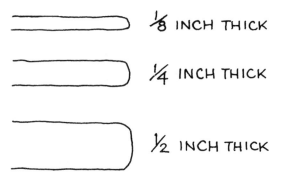

$\frac{1}{8}$ INCH THICK

$\frac{1}{4}$ INCH THICK

$\frac{1}{2}$ INCH THICK

After you've rolled out the dough evenly, dip a cookie cutter into the flour and press the cutter down very firmly on the dough. Then lift the cutter, move it over, and cut another cookie. Try not to leave space between the cookies. If you don't have cookie cutters just use a drinking glass or a small, sharp pointed knife to cut the dough.

Lift the cut-out cookies one at a time with a pancake turner or spatula, pick them up, and transfer to a baking sheet. Take the leftover scraps of dough and push them together into a ball. Roll out the dough again and cut more cookies. Sometimes cut-out cookies are filled or folded or shaped before being baked.

Bar Cookies: After you've mixed the dough put it in a baking pan and spread it out evenly with a rubber spatula. After it's baked, cut it into squares or bars while it's still in the pan, as you do when you make brownies. In some recipes the dough is chilled, not baked, before it is cut into bars.

Griddle Cakes or Pancakes: Usually griddle cakes or pancakes are rolled out and cut with a cookie cutter. (See *Roll and Cut Cookies* for details.) Put a pancake griddle on the stove and heat it a little over a medium flame. Depending on the recipe, melt butter or lard on the griddle. Then pick up the cookies with a pancake turner and lay them on the griddle a few at a time and cook them on one side. Turn them over and cook them on the other side.

Fried Cookies: When you make fried cookies always ask an adult to help you. It's best not to try fried cookies until you've learned to make other kinds first. The dough for fried cookies may be rolled and cut or shaped; or it may just be dropped by spoonfuls into the hot oil. Pour some oil into a heavy frying pan, heavy saucepan, wok (a Chinese frying pan with a round bottom), or deep fryer and let it heat up slowly. When the oil is hot enough that you can see little movements on its surface, but not so hot that it smokes, drop in the cookies a few at a time and let them cook until they're as brown as the recipe says they should be. The oil shouldn't be so hot that the cookies burn. You'll probably have to lower the flame as you cook, because the oil will keep getting hotter. When the cookies are done take them out of the hot oil with tongs and lay them on paper towels so that the extra oil can drain off. When you've finished making the cookies turn off the stove and let the oil *cool completely* before removing the pan from the stove. Always use potholders when you hold the pan or remove it from the stove.

Cupcakes: After you've mixed the batter spoon it into greased or greased and floured cupcake tins or special tins mentioned in the recipe. Put in only as much batter as the recipe tells you, because the cupcakes rise and fill the tins as they bake.

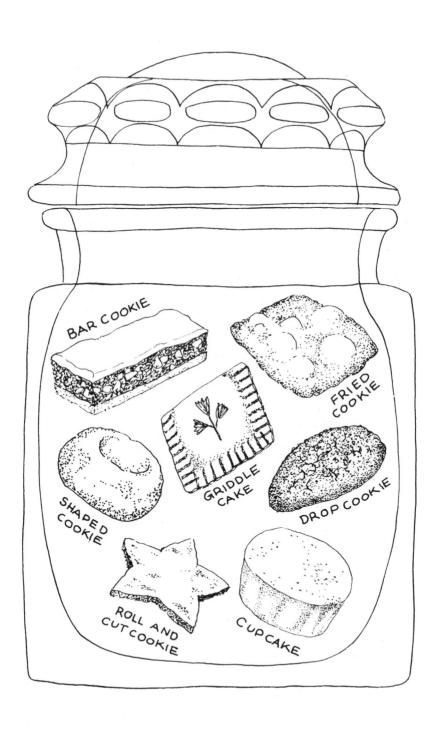

BAR COOKIE

FRIED COOKIE

GRIDDLE CAKE

SHAPED COOKIE

DROP COOKIE

ROLL AND CUT COOKIE

CUPCAKE

THESE ARE SOME OF THE UTENSILS YOU'LL BE USING

SIFTER

WOK

MIXING BOWLS

SAUCEPANS

GRIDDLE

KETTLE

COLANDER

FRYING PAN

DOUBLE BOILER

DEEP FRYER

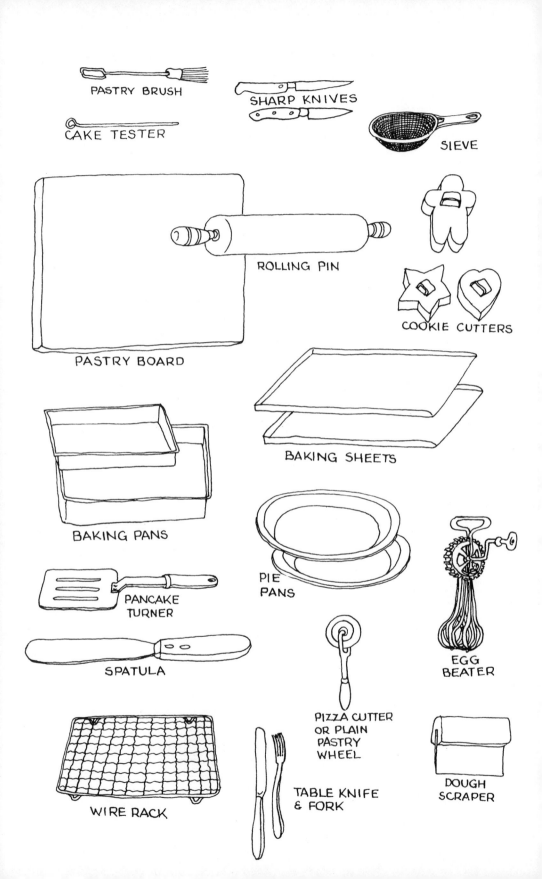

PASTRY BRUSH

SHARP KNIVES

CAKE TESTER

SIEVE

ROLLING PIN

COOKIE CUTTERS

PASTRY BOARD

BAKING SHEETS

BAKING PANS

PIE PANS

PANCAKE TURNER

SPATULA

EGG BEATER

WIRE RACK

PIZZA CUTTER OR PLAIN PASTRY WHEEL

TABLE KNIFE & FORK

DOUGH SCRAPER

GRATER

PASTRY BLENDER

MEASURING CUPS & SPOONS

CUSTARD CUPS

POTATO MASHER

TONGS

WIRE WHISK

JUICER

NUT CHOPPER

POTATO PEELER

RUBBER SPATULA

SKIMMER

SLOTTED SPOON

MEAT GRINDER

MORTAR & PESTLE

COOKING SPOONS

FOOD MILL

YOU'LL FIND SOME OF THESE DIRECTIONS IN ALL COOKIE RECIPES

Preheat Oven: Set the oven dial at the temperature mentioned in the recipe and turn the oven on about ten or fifteen minutes before you're ready to bake. Then the oven will be just the right temperature when you're ready to put in the cookies. Always ask an adult for permission to turn on the oven.

Measure the Diameter: To find the diameter or width of a round object, such as a baking pan or cookie cutter, measure across the object at its widest part. For instance, this is a cookie cutter 3 inches in diameter.

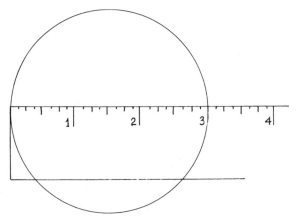

Cream: To soften butter, margarine, or other shortening place it in a bowl and work it against the inside of the bowl with a spoon, stirring until it is soft and creamy.

Blanch Almonds: Blanched almonds are almonds with the shells and brown skins removed. You can buy packaged blanched almonds either whole or slivered. To blanch almonds yourself, first remove the shells (if any) with a nutcracker. Place the almonds in a small bowl and pour in boiling water to just cover the nuts. Let them stand two minutes. Drain off the water and cover the nuts with cold water. Take the almonds, one at a time, and squeeze between your thumb and index finger until the brown skins pop off. Pat the almonds dry in paper towels.

Blend or Combine: To mix two or more ingredients together well with a spoon.

Cut In: To distribute butter or other shortening in dry ingredients, use a pastry blender and push it down and through the butter and flour; or work the ingredients together with your fingertips. Either way, keep doing this over and over, until the mixture becomes crumbly.

Beat: To use an egg beater or wire whisk or a spoon to stir with a quick steady motion that lifts the ingredients over and over until they are smooth. See also *Beat Egg Whites, Yolks, or Whole Eggs.*

Chop: If you don't have a nut chopper, put the ingredients, usually nuts, on a cutting board or pastry board and cut through them over and over with a large sharp knife that has a flat 6- to 8-inch blade, until you have the desired consistency. One hand should hold the knife handle, and the other should hold the top edge of the blade.

Fold: To combine two ingredients or mixtures (one of which is usually beaten egg whites), push a rubber spatula straight down through the center of the ingredients and bring it toward the side of the bowl and up to the top so that the ingredients begin to fold, or combine. Then turn the bowl around a little bit and do the same thing again with the rubber spatula. Do this very gently and keep doing it until the mixture in the bowl looks even.

Grind: You can buy some nuts already ground, especially almonds. To grind your own nuts, first remove the shells (if any) with a nutcracker. Put the nutmeats through a hand-operated meat grinder with a medium blade. Then put them through the meat grinder with a fine blade. Measure them after you've ground them.

Measure: To put an ingredient into a measuring cup or measuring spoon so that it is filled evenly to the amount the recipe calls for.

Grate: To grate orange or lemon peel set the grater on a piece of waxed paper, hold the grater with one hand, and rub the fruit against its fine side. Make sure not to grate any of the white part of the rind because it has a bitter taste. To grate cheese use the coarse side of the grater, and be careful with your fingers when you get near the end of the cheese.

Measure and Sift Dry Ingredients: Measure flour or confectioners' sugar by piling it lightly into a measuring cup without pressing it down. Then push off the extra flour or sugar evenly with a metal spatula or table knife. *To sift,* set the sifter on a piece of waxed paper, and put the flour or sugar into the sifter. Hold the sifter over the waxed paper and sift the flour or sugar onto it.

Sift Together: Set the sifter on a piece of waxed paper. Measure all the ingredients to be sifted (such as flour, baking powder, salt, and spices) and put them into the sifter. Then sift them all together onto the waxed paper.

Break an Egg: Crack the eggshell on the edge of a cup, and let the egg fall into the cup while you hold onto the two pieces of shell. Throw away the shell.

Separate an Egg: When recipes ask you to use either the white or yolk of an egg, crack the shell on the edge of a cup and hold the egg over it, turning the separate halves upward like two little bowls. As you do so, let the white part fall into the cup and keep the yolk in the other half of the eggshell. Put the yolk in another cup. If you're going to separate more than one egg, hold each egg over a separate cup when you break it. Then if the yolk should break it won't spoil the eggs you've already separated. Ask an adult to show you how to separate an egg the first time.

Beat Egg Whites, Yolks, or Whole Eggs: When using an egg beater (also called a rotary beater) hold it up straight in the bowl and turn the handle as quickly as you can. If you use a wire whisk use a quick, steady down, up, and over motion that lifts the eggs over and over to get as much air into them as you can.

Sauté: To cook something in a small amount of oil or butter in a frying pan over medium low flame.

Knead Dough: To make dough smooth and even by working it with your hands, press it with the heels of your hands, fold it, turn it, and press again. Keep doing this for a few minutes, or as long as the recipe tells you. Sometimes you can knead right in the bowl, and other times it's easier to take the dough out of the bowl and knead it on a floured pastry board.

Butter or Grease a Baking Sheet: Put a little butter or other shortening on a paper towel and rub it lightly and evenly all over the inside of a baking sheet.

Flour a Baking Sheet: After you butter the baking sheet sprinkle a spoonful or two of flour over the buttered part. Tap the baking sheet on the table, tilting it at the same time so the flour covers the butter completely. Then hold the baking sheet upside down over the sink and give it a sharp tap on the bottom to knock off any extra flour.

Bake: To cook in the oven. Arrange the oven shelf so it will be near the center of the oven before you turn the oven on.

Remove from Oven and Baking Sheet, and Cool on Wire Rack: Use potholders to take the baking sheet out of the oven. Slide a pancake turner or spatula under the cookies to loosen them from the baking sheet, and put them on a wire rack so they aren't touching each other. The air will circulate around them to cool them.

SPECIAL INGREDIENTS

Ammonium Carbonate (Hartshorn): A white powder that acts like baking powder to make cookies and cakes rise in baking. You can buy it for a few cents at your drugstore.

Barley Flour: A flour ground from hulled barley, rather than wheat. You can buy it at health food stores and at some supermarkets.

Cake Flour: A fine white flour made from soft wheat that gives cookies and other baked goods a finer, more crumbly texture. You can buy cake flour in any supermarket.

Hartshorn or Hartshorn Salt: See *Ammonium Carbonate.*

Orange Flower Water: A fragrant liquid made by distilling orange blossoms in water. It's used primarily for flavoring baked goods and desserts. You can buy it in stores where Middle Eastern, Greek, French, or Portuguese people shop, or you can buy it in specialty food shops.

Poppyseed Filling, Lekvar (Prune Butter), and Apricot Butter: These items can be bought in supermarkets, groceries, and specialty food shops.

Rice Flour: A flour ground from white rice. You can buy it in Oriental food stores or in specialty food shops.

Rose Water: A delicately scented liquid made by distilling fragrant rose petals in water. It's used mostly in baked goods and desserts. You can buy it in Greek or Middle Eastern food stores, or in specialty food shops and some supermarkets.

SOME COOKIE-MAKING TIPS

 Read the recipe all the way through so you'll understand it. Check to see if you have all the ingredients, so you can shop, if necessary.

 Ask if it's all right to use the kitchen, and set out all the ingredients and utensils you will need before you start to mix the dough.

If you need cookies in a hurry don't choose a recipe in which the dough has to sit overnight before baking.

Leave plenty of space between the cookies when you put them on the baking sheet because they usually spread out while they're baking.

You can put one or two baking sheets in the oven at a time, but be sure to put them on the same oven shelf so they'll bake evenly.

Don't put cookie dough on a hot baking sheet. If you have to use the same baking sheet twice let it cool off in between.

Always use potholders to take baking sheets out of the oven, and whenever you work with pans on the stove.

After you've enjoyed some of the cookies remember to clean up the kitchen.

You can freeze any of the cookies in this book except griddle cakes, pancakes, fried cookies, or cookies that are soaked in syrup. To freeze cookies, allow them to cool completely after baking. Wrap the cookies tightly in plastic wrap, or pack them closely in a plastic container with a tight-fitting lid. You can keep them for as long as two months in your freezer.

Cookies from Europe and Eastern Europe

Austria

ALMOND CRESCENTS
KIPFERLN

(KEEP-ferln)

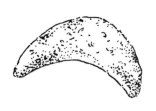

In the eighteenth century the coffeehouses of Vienna, Austria, were noted for the variety of delicious pastries they made and served. People met at the coffeehouses, or cafes, not only to gossip, flirt, exchange news, and debate politics but also to taste some of the world's finest baking and to drink from a wide selection of coffees. *Kipferln* are typical of some of the cookies served in the coffeehouses, and are still popular in Austria today. Their shape represents the crescent moon on the flag of Turkey, in honor of an Austrian military victory over the Turks.

INGREDIENTS:

1⅓ cups cake flour (see page 24)	½ cup (1 stick) sweet butter
2 tablespoons sugar	1 teaspoon vanilla extract
⅓ cup ground blanched almonds (see page 20)	1 cup confectioners' sugar

UTENSILS: mixing bowl, sifter, measuring cups and spoons, cooking spoon, table knife, baking sheets, spatula or pancake turner, wire rack, sieve, shallow bowl.

METHOD: Shaped cookies (see page 13).

Preheat oven at 350°. Sift together into mixing bowl the flour and 2 tablespoons sugar. Add the ground blanched almonds and mix together.

Cut the butter into small pieces and add to the flour mixture. With your fingers mix and rub the ingredients together until well blended. Add the vanilla extract and mix in with your fingers until well blended and smooth.

Pull off pieces of dough and roll between the palms of your hands into balls about 1 inch in diameter. Roll the balls into long ovals, and then shape them with your fingers into crescents (quarter moon shapes). Arrange on ungreased baking sheets.

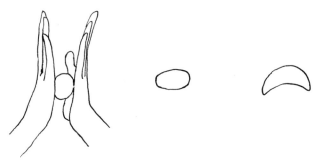

Bake 12 to 15 minutes until lightly browned. Remove from oven and baking sheets, and cool slightly on wire rack. Into a shallow bowl sift confectioners' sugar, and roll the cookies in the sugar while they are still warm. Put them back on wire rack to cool completely.

Makes about 2 dozen.

Belgium

MIRRORS
SPECULAAS

(SPAY-koo-lahs)

The most popular cookie in Belgium, particularly western Belgium, is *Speculaas,* a rectangular cookie stamped with windmills, animals, St. Nicholas, or other designs. Belgian children especially look forward to having these cookies on St. Nicholas's Day, which comes on December 5, several weeks before Christmas. The people of Holland and Germany also bake *Speculaas* at holiday time. All these people use special wooden molds to shape the cookies. The molds have designs carved on them, and since the cookies show, or "reflect," the exact patterns of the rectangular molds they are called *Speculaas,* or "mirrors." *Speculaas* will taste good even if you have no wooden molds. Just roll out the dough and cut rectangular cookies as we do here.

INGREDIENTS:

grated rind of 1 lemon
   (see page 22)
¾ cup (1½ sticks) butter
   or margarine
½ cup white sugar
½ cup dark brown sugar
2¼ cups flour
1 teaspoon baking soda
1½ teaspoons nutmeg

1½ teaspoons cinnamon
1½ teaspoons ground
   coriander
¾ teaspoon ground cloves
¼ teaspoon white pepper
1 teaspoon salt
2 tablespoons milk

UTENSILS: grater, baking sheets, mixing bowl, measuring cups and spoons, cooking spoons, waxed paper, sifter, pastry board, rolling pin, small sharp knife or 2-inch by 3-inch rectangular cookie cutter, spatula or pancake turner, wire rack.

METHOD: Roll and cut cookies (see page 14).

Grease baking sheets. Grate the lemon rind on a piece of waxed paper. In a mixing bowl cream the butter or margarine until soft. Add the white sugar and dark brown sugar and mix well. Add the grated lemon rind.

Onto a piece of waxed paper sift together the flour, baking soda, nutmeg, cinnamon, coriander, cloves, white pepper, and salt. Gradually add to the butter and sugar mixture and mix well. Add the milk and mix well with your hands.

Preheat oven at 350°. Knead the dough for 5 minutes to make it smooth. Sprinkle some flour on pastry board and roll out the dough with a floured rolling pin, until it is about ¼ inch thick. Cut into rectangles about 2 inches by 3 inches using a small sharp knife to cut through the dough, or use a rectangular cookie cutter. Arrange cookies on baking sheets. Bake about 10 minutes. Remove from oven and baking sheets, and cool on wire rack.
Makes about 3 dozen.

Denmark

COCONUT DREAMS
KOKOSDRØMME

(KAW-kaws-drawm-meh)

This recipe calls for two unusual ingredients which you can buy at your drugstore. One is cocoa butter, made from the seed of the cocoa bean, from which we also get chocolate and cocoa. The other ingredient is ammonium carbonate, sometimes called hartshorn or hartshorn salt. It's an ingredient similar to baking powder which makes baked goods rise in the oven, and is used in many European countries. Hartshorn was used in our country, too, in colonial times. But when we invented baking powder and began to produce it commercially Americans stopped using hartshorn almost completely. Hartshorn gives food a crisper texture than baking powder, which has never become popular in Europe, particularly in northern countries like Denmark.

INGREDIENTS:
2 ounces cocoa butter
¼ cup (half a stick) butter
*   or margarine*
⅓ cup sugar
1 cup unsweetened flaked
*   coconut*

1 cup flour
¾ teaspoon ammonium
*   carbonate (see page 24)*

UTENSILS: small saucepan, wooden spoon, mixing bowl, measuring cups and spoons, waxed paper, sifter, baking sheets, spatula or pancake turner, wire rack.

METHOD: Shaped cookies (see page 13).

Preheat oven at 300°. Put the cocoa butter in a small saucepan and set over a low flame. As the cocoa butter melts, stir slowly with a wooden spoon, and remove from heat as soon as it's completely melted.

In a mixing bowl cream the butter or margarine until soft. Pour in the cocoa butter and mix together. Add the sugar and mix thoroughly, pressing lumps against the sides of the bowl, until the dough is very smooth. Then add the coconut and mix well.

Onto a piece of waxed paper sift together the flour and ammonium carbonate. If the sifter contains any lumps of ammonium carbonate turn them out onto a board and crush them with the back of a spoon until they are powdered. Then sift them again with the flour. Gradually add the sifted mixture to the butter, mixing well each time. When all the flour has been added mix well with your hands until the dough is smooth and even. The ammonium carbonate may give the dough an odd smell, but the odor will disappear during the baking.

Take small pieces of dough and squeeze and shape between your palms into little balls about the size of a large marble. Arrange on ungreased baking sheets. Bake 25 to 30 minutes until lightly browned. Remove from oven and baking sheets, and cool on wire rack.

Makes 2½ to 3 dozen.

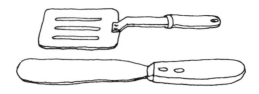

England

COVENTRY GODCAKES

Children living around Coventry and Warwickshire in England are given Coventry Godcakes by their godparents on New Year's Day, or to celebrate the children's birthdays. The cakes are actually triangular tarts filled with mincemeat. Sometimes they're baked in sizes as large as 18 inches wide.

INGREDIENTS:

1 cup flour
  pinch of salt
½ cup water
½ cup (1 stick) butter or
    margarine

1 jar mincemeat (about
    14 ounces)
1 egg white
  sugar

UTENSILS: mixing bowl, measuring cups and spoons, cooking spoons, pastry board, rolling pin, sharp knife with 6-inch blade, ruler, flat dinner plate, baking sheets, small sharp knife or pizza cutter or plain pastry wheel, 2 cups, small bowl, egg beater or wire whisk, pastry brush, spatula or pancake turner, wire rack.

METHOD: Roll and cut cookies (see page 14).

In a mixing bowl combine flour and salt. Add the water and mix until well combined. Sprinkle a little flour on the pastry board and knead the dough on the board for 5 minutes.

With a floured rolling pin roll out the dough into a large rectangle about 13 or 14 inches long and 7 inches wide. Use a ruler to measure the dough. You will have to do a lot of pushing to make the dough roll out, because it will keep springing back. Just keep rolling to make it stretch out.

Take the stick of butter from the refrigerator and cut it into 4 long thin slices with a sharp knife, like this:

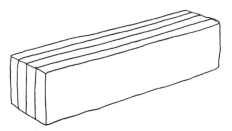

Run the knife blade under hot water each time before you cut the butter, and it will cut more easily.

Lay the butter slices on the dough so that it looks like this.

Then fold the dough over the butter and press the edges together with your fingers. Sprinkle a little flour over the dough, and wipe more flour on the rolling pin. Then roll out the dough with the butter in it until you have a rectangle about 7 inches by 12 inches.

Then fold it into thirds like this:

Roll the folded dough out again to a rectangle about 7 inches by 12 inches. Then fold it into thirds again. Put the dough on a dinner plate and put it in the refrigerator 15 minutes.

Preheat oven at 425°. Grease baking sheets. Remove dough from refrigerator. Sprinkle a little flour on the pastry board, and roll out the dough to a rectangle 10 inches by 18 inches. With a pizza cutter, pastry wheel, or small sharp knife, cut the dough into 8 parts, see below. Then cut each part in half to make triangles, see below. Arrange 8 dough triangles on baking sheets. Put a spoonful of mincemeat in the center of each triangle.

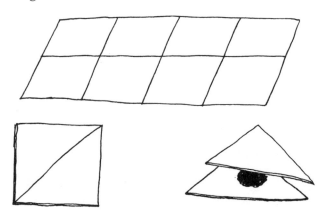

Put some cold water from the faucet in a cup, and dip your finger into it to moisten all around the edge of each triangle. Then put the remaining triangles on top of the mincemeat, and press the edges together with your fingers. Make a little slit in the top of each triangle with a small sharp knife.

Bake 12 to 15 minutes until lightly browned. While the Godcakes are baking, separate an egg. Put the egg yolk in a cup and save for another use. Put the egg white in a small bowl and beat slightly with an egg beater or wire whisk. When the Godcakes are lightly browned, remove baking sheets from oven. Using a pastry brush, brush some egg white over each Godcake. With your fingers sprinkle a little sugar over each one. Return baking sheets to the oven for 3 minutes. Remove from oven and baking sheets, and cool on wire rack. **Makes 8.**

France

SHELL-SHAPED BUTTER CAKES
MADELEINES

(MA-dlehn)

Many years ago in France the dough that is now associated exclusively with *Madeleines* was often used to make cakes and pastries in other shapes. Then in the nineteenth century a famous French pastry cook, named Avice, decided to bake the dough in little shell-shaped forms. He named them *Madeleines*. Now *Madeleines* are one of France's most popular cookies, or little cakes. In order to make them you'll need to buy a *Madeleine* tin in a housewares or specialty cookware store.

INGREDIENTS:

½ cup (1 stick) butter
½ cup sugar
1 cup cake flour
    (see page 24)
2 eggs

pinch of salt
½ teaspoon grated lemon
    rind
2 or 3 tablespoons
    confectioners' sugar

UTENSILS: Madeleine tin, grater, waxed paper, small saucepan, measuring cups and spoons, sifter, cooking spoons, mixing bowl, cake tester, wire rack, sieve.

METHOD: Cupcakes (see page 15).

Preheat the oven at 350°. Grease and flour the *Madeleine* tin. Grate the lemon rind on a piece of waxed paper.

   Put the butter in saucepan and set over a low flame until melted. Remove from stove and set aside to cool.

   Sift cake flour onto a piece of waxed paper. Measure and place in mixing bowl. Add the sugar, salt, and grated lemon rind and toss together. Add the eggs and mix well. Add the melted butter and mix well.

Spoon the dough into *Madeleine* tin until it's just a little more than half full. Bake 15 to 20 minutes, or until a cake tester inserted through the thickest part comes out clean. Remove tin from oven, remove *Madeleines* from tin, and cool on wire rack.

Put tin in a pan of cold water to cool it. Then wash it with hot water and soap, dry it, and grease and flour it as you did before. Finish baking the rest of the dough. When all *Madeleines* are baked put the confectioners' sugar in a sieve, and sift it over them.

Makes about 1½ dozen.

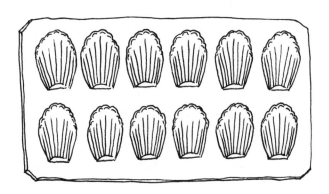

MADELEINE TIN

Germany

CINNAMON STARS
ZIMTSTERNE

(TSIM-shter-neh)

Christmas is baking and candy-making time in Germany. Marzipan, a brightly colored, almond-flavored confection, is made into all kinds of shapes—pigs, angels, snowmen, poodles, bananas, and even fried eggs. Bread is baked in Santa Claus shapes, and the cakes, pastries, and cookies are endless. Some of the best known Christmas cookies are *Lebkuchen,* honey spice cookies that are often made in heart shapes; *Pfeffernusse,* or "peppernuts," which are spicy little cookies dusted with sugar; *Springerle,* pale white picture cookies; and *Zimtsterne,* or "cinnamon stars," which you can make from this recipe.

INGREDIENTS:
2 egg whites
½ cup superfine sugar
¼ teaspoon almond extract
½ cup cake flour
   (see page 24)

1½ teaspoons cinnamon
1 cup ground almonds
   (see page 21)
1 cup superfine sugar
1 egg white

UTENSILS: cup, mixing bowl, egg beater, measuring cups and spoons, cooking spoons, waxed paper, sifter, rubber spatula, pastry board, rolling pin, baking sheets, small bowl, pastry brush, star-shaped cookie cutter, spatula or pancake turner, wire rack.

METHOD: Roll and cut cookies (see page 14).

Separate 2 eggs. Put the yolks in a cup and save for another use. Put the whites in a mixing bowl and beat with an egg beater until foamy. Add the ½ cup superfine sugar gradually, and continue beating the mixture with the egg beater until it is very thick. Add the almond extract and stir with a spoon.

Onto a piece of waxed paper sift together the cake flour and cinnamon. Add the flour mixture and the ground almonds to the egg white mixture, and fold in carefully with a rubber spatula. Set bowl in the refrigerator for 30 minutes.

Sprinkle the 1 cup superfine sugar on the pastry board. Take the dough from the bowl and set it on the sugar. Place a large piece of waxed paper over it. With a rolling pin roll out the covered dough, until it is about ¼ inch thick. Peel off the waxed paper and let the dough sit for 30 minutes.

Preheat oven at 300°. Grease baking sheets. Separate 1 egg and add the yolk to the yolks you have already set aside. Put the egg white in a small bowl and beat lightly with the egg beater until it just begins to get foamy.

Cut out the cookies with a star-shaped cookie cutter, and arrange on baking sheets. Using a pastry brush, brush each star with some of the egg white. Bake 25 minutes. Remove from oven and baking sheets, and cool on wire rack.
Makes about 3 dozen.

Iceland

HALF-MOONS
HÁLFMÁNAR

(HALF-ma-nahr)

Half-Moons are traditional Icelandic cookies that are especially popular at Christmas time. An ingredient in these cookies that may not be familiar to you is cardamom, a fragrant spice popular in Scandinavian countries. Cardamom was first brought to Iceland by the Vikings, who were introduced to the flavor when their sailing expeditions took them to Middle Eastern spice trading centers many hundreds of years ago.

INGREDIENTS:

2½ cups flour
⅔ cup sugar
½ teaspoon baking powder
*1 teaspoon ground
    cardamom*
*½ teaspoon ammonium
    carbonate (see page 24)*

1⅓ cups butter or margarine
1 egg
*1 10-ounce jar prune
    butter (lekvar)*

UTENSILS: sifter, mixing bowl, measuring cups and spoons, table knife, small bowl, egg beater or wire whisk, cooking spoons, baking sheets, pastry board, rolling pin, round cookie cutter or drinking glass, table fork, spatula or pancake turner, wire rack.

METHOD: Roll and cut cookies (see page 14).

Sift together into mixing bowl the flour, sugar, baking powder, cardamom, and ammonium carbonate. Cut the butter into small pieces and add to the flour mixture. Work the ingredients together with your fingers until well blended.

In a small bowl beat the egg lightly with an egg beater or wire whisk, and add to the dough. Mix well with a spoon. Place the bowl in refrigerator 1 hour to chill.

Preheat oven at 350°. Grease baking sheets. Sprinkle some flour on the pastry board and place the dough on it. With a floured rolling pin roll dough out to about ¼ inch thickness or less. Cut out circles with a round cookie cutter or the rim of a drinking glass. Arrange on baking sheets. Put ½ teaspoon prune butter, or lekvar, on each cookie. Fold cookies over to cover filling and form half-moon shapes. With a fork press edges of cookies together firmly, making fork marks on the rounded edges. Bake 10 to 11 minutes. Remove from oven and baking sheets, and cool on wire rack.
Makes 5 to 6 dozen.

Ireland
OATCAKES

Oats are grown on Irish farms and are a favorite cereal there. Irish oatmeal is a sturdy breakfast dish, and oatcakes are often eaten throughout the day. In olden days oatcakes were set to bake on little stands placed directly over glowing coals in the fireplace. Now they're baked in the oven, as in this recipe. Oatcakes are hard and crunchy, and eating them can be good exercise for your teeth. Try your oatcakes with butter and with some jam, honey, or cheese.

INGREDIENTS:

½ cup flour	1¾ cup rolled oats
1 teaspoon cream of tartar	(uncooked)
1½ teaspoons salt	⅓ cup boiling water
⅛ teaspoon baking soda	2 teaspoons vegetable oil

UTENSILS: 2 baking sheets, sifter, mixing bowl, measuring cups and spoons, cooking spoons, teakettle or small saucepan, pastry board, rolling pin, sharp knife, spatula.

METHOD: Roll and cut cookies (see page 14).

Preheat oven at 325°. Sprinkle a little flour on the baking sheets. Sift together into a mixing bowl the flour, cream of tartar, salt, and baking soda. Add the rolled oats and toss together.

Boil a cup of water in teakettle or saucepan and measure ⅓ cup. Holding the cup with a potholder, add the boiling water to the oatmeal mixture, and mix well. Add the vegetable oil and mix well. If the dough is too dry and will not hold together add 1 more tablespoon of boiling water. Divide the dough into two equal parts.

Sprinkle a few spoonfuls of rolled oats on the pastry board. Put one part of the dough on the rolled oats, and roll it out as thin as you can with a floured rolling pin, keeping the shape as round as you can. Then cut with a sharp knife into 8 wedges like a pie. Transfer the wedges to a baking sheet with a spatula. Roll out the other part of the dough, cut it into wedges, and transfer the wedges to the other baking sheet.

Bake about 25 minutes until centers are dry and edges are lightly browned. Remove from oven and baking sheets. Butter cakes and eat right away, or eat them later cold or reheated in the toaster.

Makes 16.

Italy

ALMOND MACAROONS
AMARETTI

(ah-mah-REH-tee)

Amaretti, which are made from almond paste, have been popular in Italy for at least four hundred years. There are several large almond-producing areas in Italy, so it seems only natural that a cookie like *Amaretti* was created there. When Catherine de Medici, an aristocratic young Italian, left her country in the sixteenth century to marry the future king of France, she took along her pastry cooks and the *Amaretti* recipe, and introduced the cookie to the French. In Italian *Amaretti* means "little bitter ones," so the ancient cookies were apparently made with very little sugar and probably contained some bitter almonds along with the sweet ones.

INGREDIENTS:

1 cup almond paste	*1 cup sugar*
(8-ounce package or	*½ cup flour*
can)	*pinch of salt*
3 egg whites	*sugar*

UTENSILS: baking sheets, aluminum foil, measuring cups, 2 mixing bowls, wooden spoon, cup, egg beater or wire whisk, sifter, waxed paper, wire rack.

METHOD: Drop cookies (see page 13).

Preheat oven at 300°. Cut off a piece of aluminum foil long enough to cover the bottom of baking sheet. Lay it smoothly in the baking sheet. Do the same with other baking sheet or sheets.

Put almond paste in a mixing bowl, and with your hands or a wooden spoon break it up and work it until it is smooth and soft.

Separate the eggs. Put the yolks in a cup and save for another use. Put the whites in a mixing bowl and beat them lightly with an egg beater or wire whisk until they just begin to get foamy. Add the egg whites to the almond paste and blend thoroughly. Gradually add 1 cup sugar and mix well.

Onto a sheet of waxed paper sift the flour. Measure it and sift it together with the salt. Add to the almond mixture and mix well.

Drop by teaspoonfuls onto the foil-lined baking sheets, making shallow mounds about 1 inch in diameter. Sprinkle lightly with sugar. Bake about 20 minutes. Remove from oven and foil-lined baking sheets, and cool on wire rack.
Makes about 2½ dozen.

Netherlands

GOSSIP HEADS
KLETSKOPPEN

(KLEHTS-kaw-pn)

In Dutch *Kletskoppen* means "gossip heads." These cookies are called this because they are the kind of cookie that is often served at afternoon tea where people get together to chat and gossip. *Kletskoppen* should be very dry, thin, and brittle. They don't like damp weather, so remember to make them on a day when it isn't raining.

INGREDIENTS:

¼ cup finely chopped blanched almonds (see page 20)

¼ cup (half a stick) butter or margarine

1 cup light brown sugar, loosely packed

⅓ cup flour

1 tablespoon water

UTENSILS: *baking sheets, cutting board and sharp knife with 6- to 8-inch blade or nut chopper, measuring cups and spoons, mixing bowl, cooking spoons, spatula or pancake turner, wire rack.*

METHOD: Drop cookies (see page 13).

Preheat oven at 300°. Grease baking sheets. Chop almonds finely. Cream the butter in a mixing bowl until soft. Add the brown sugar gradually and mix well. Add the flour and mix until thoroughly blended. Add the finely chopped almonds and the water and mix well.

Drop by teaspoonfuls on baking sheets, baking only 6 cookies at a time on a sheet. Allow at least 3 inches between each cookie, because they spread out a lot as they bake. Bake 13 to 14 minutes. Remove baking sheets from oven and leave

cookies on sheets for several minutes to harden. Remove cookies from baking sheets and cool on wire rack. If the cookies become too brittle to remove from the baking sheet, just put the baking sheet back in the oven for a minute.
Makes 2 dozen.

Portugal

SPONGE CAKES
PÃO DE LÓ
(PAH-oo dih LAW)

In Portugal egg yolk sweets are the most typical of all desserts. Custards, puddings, and cakes all have a bright yellow color from the many egg yolks used in them. This practice began centuries ago when nuns, experimenting with many kinds of complicated egg yolk desserts, became famous for their recipes and their skill in making them. Today, the most difficult egg yolk sweets are rarely made at home and are generally bought by the Portuguese in bakeries. *Pão de Ló*, however, are easy to make and are one of the most popular egg yolk cakes in Portugal. *Pão de Ló* can be baked in large round tube pans, loaf pans, or in cupcake tins such as we use in this recipe.

INGREDIENTS:

3 egg yolks	*5 tablespoons sugar*
1 egg	*6 tablespoons cake flour*
pinch of salt	

UTENSILS: waxed paper, drinking glass about 2¾ inches in diameter, pencil, scissors, 2 very small 12-place cupcake tins, mixing bowl, cups, egg beater, measuring cups and spoons, sifter, small spoon, wire rack.

METHOD: Cupcakes (see page 15).

Use a drinking glass as a guide to trace 24 circles on a sheet of waxed paper. Cut circles out with scissors. Butter the circles on one side. Butter the cupcake tins very heavily and place circles in them, buttered side up. Pat circles into place so the waxed paper lies smoothly against bottom and sides of tins.

Preheat oven at 325°. Separate 3 eggs and put yolks in the mixing bowl. Put the whites in a cup and save for another use. Break the remaining egg into the mixing bowl with the yolks. Add the salt and beat with an egg beater for several minutes until thick. Add the sugar gradually, beating well each time, until mixture is very thick. Sift the flour onto a sheet of waxed paper. Add flour to the egg mixture gradually and beat until mixture is smooth.

Spoon the batter into the prepared cupcake tins, filling them about two-thirds full. Bake 13 or 14 minutes until light brown. Remove from oven and cupcake tins and cool on wire rack. **Makes 24.**

Scotland

SHORTBREAD

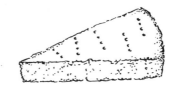

The Scots are famous for their shortbread, which they made in olden times with fine oat flour and butter. Through the years there has been a gradual change to wheat flour, usually mixed with rice flour. However, the importance of butter in the recipe has never changed. Since there are only a few ingredients in shortbread, most of the flavor comes from the butter, so never substitute margarine. There's never any salt in genuine Scotch shortbread, so buy sweet (unsalted) butter. The word *short* in shortbread means that it contains a lot of shortening (butter), which makes it break and crumble easily. This is the sign of a good shortbread.

INGREDIENTS:
½ cup (1 stick) sweet butter   *½ cup rice flour (see*
¼ cup sugar   *page 24)*
1 cup flour

UTENSILS: mixing bowl, measuring cups and spoons, cooking spoons, waxed paper, sifter, 9-inch pie pan, table fork, sharp knife, spatula, wire rack.

METHOD: Shaped cookies (see page 13).

Preheat oven at 350°. Cream butter in mixing bowl until soft. Add sugar gradually and mix well. Onto a piece of waxed paper sift the flour and rice flour. Gradually add to the butter mixture, mixing well. Spoon the dough into the ungreased pie pan, and with the back of a spoon press it down smoothly and evenly over the bottom of the pan. Smooth the edges with your fingers. With the tines of a fork make rows of fork pricks on the dough about every ½ inch.

Bake 25 to 30 minutes until light gold. Remove from oven. Using a sharp knife, cut into 8 wedges. With a spatula remove wedges from the pie pan, and cool on wire rack.
Makes 8.

Spain

ST. JOSEPH'S WOOD SHAVINGS
VIRUTILLAS DE SAN JOSÉ

(vee-roo-TEE-yahs deh sahn hoe-SAY)

In Spain they make *Virutillas* on March 18 to celebrate St. Joseph's Day. The cookies resemble the curled wood shavings that fell to the floor when Joseph of Nazareth worked in his carpenter's shop. Spaniards wrap thin strands of dough around a special kind of stick and fry them to form cookies, which taste very good, and not at all like wood shavings. We wrap our dough around ice cream pop sticks, so save as many as you can for *Virutilla*-baking day.

INGREDIENTS:

3 *tablespoons butter*
3 *tablespoons lard*
¼ *cup sugar*
1 *egg*
1½ *teaspoons port wine (or any other sweet wine)*
¼ *teaspoon grated lemon rind*
½ *teaspoon grated orange rind*
1½ *cups flour*
   big pinch of cinnamon
   vegetable oil
½ *cup confectioners' sugar*

UTENSILS: grater, waxed paper, mixing bowl, small bowl, measuring cups and spoons, cooking spoons, egg beater or wire whisk, sifter, ice cream sticks (as many as 24), heavy frying pan, tongs, paper towels, sieve.

METHOD: Fried cookies (see page 15).

Grate the lemon rind and orange rind onto a piece of waxed paper. In a mixing bowl cream the butter and lard together until soft. Add sugar gradually and beat until fluffy. In small bowl beat the egg lightly and add it to the butter-sugar mixture. Stir in the port wine, grated lemon and orange rinds, and mix well. Sift the flour and cinnamon onto a piece of waxed paper. Gradually add to the egg mixture and mix well, first with a spoon, and then with your hands, until the dough is very smooth and well combined.

Pull off small pieces of dough and roll between the palms of your hands to form ropes about as fat as a thick pencil and 6 or 7 inches long.

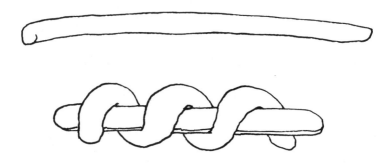

Wrap a rope of dough round and round each wooden ice cream stick so it reaches from one end to the other to form a long curl. Keep wrapping until you run out of sticks—the recipe makes about 24. If you don't have enough you can finish one batch and then do the rest.

Ask an adult to help you with the next part of this recipe. In a heavy frying pan pour vegetable oil until it's about ¾ inch deep. Place over medium flame and heat until hot, but not smoking, until you can see little movements on the surface of the oil. With tongs place the dough-wrapped sticks into the oil about 6 at a time, and let them brown very lightly on one side. This will take less than a minute. With tongs turn them over and let them brown a few seconds on the other side. With tongs remove them from the oil and drain them on paper towels, but do not remove the sticks. Continue frying until all the dough-wrapped sticks are done and draining. When they are completely cool, gently pull out the sticks. Put confectioners' sugar in a sieve and sift it over the cookies. **Makes about 2 dozen.**

Sweden

MOLASSES GINGERSNAPS
SIRAPSPEPPARKAKOR

(see-rahps-pay-pahr-KAH-koor)

Gingersnaps are one of Sweden's favorite cookies, and one for which she is famous. There are many kinds of Swedish gingersnaps—thick, paper thin, very soft, very crunchy, mild, and extra spicy. Swedes also like to make gingerbread houses at Christmas time using their favorite gingersnap dough to make the parts of the house, which they then decorate with white sugar icing. The gingersnaps in our recipe are thin, crisp, and mildly spiced. *The dough needs to rest in the refrigerator 3 days before being baked.*

INGREDIENTS:

2½ tablespoons butter or margarine	1¼ teaspoons ground ginger
⅔ cup molasses	1½ teaspoons baking soda
2¾ cups flour	2 tablespoons water
	½ cup flour

UTENSILS: small saucepan, measuring cups and spoons, mixing bowl, cooking spoon, sifter, waxed paper, small bowl, plastic wrap or aluminum foil, baking sheets, pastry board, rolling pin, round cookie cutter or drinking glass, spatula or pancake turner, wire rack.

METHOD: Roll and cut cookies (see page 14).

In small saucepan melt the butter or margarine over low heat. Pour into a mixing bowl. Add the molasses and stir well. Onto a piece of waxed paper sift together the 2¾ cups flour, ground ginger, and baking soda. Add half of the flour mixture to the molasses mixture and mix well. Add the water and mix well.

Gradually add the rest of the flour mixture and mix well. Pack the dough tightly into a small bowl. Sprinkle the ½ cup flour over the top. Cover the bowl with plastic wrap or aluminum foil and place in the refrigerator for 3 days.

After 3 days remove bowl from refrigerator. Turn the flour out of the bowl and tap the bowl to remove any flour that sticks to the dough. Keep the flour for rolling out the dough. Take the dough out of the bowl and let it sit at room temperature for 30 minutes.

Preheat oven at 350°. Grease baking sheets. Divide dough into 2 equal parts. Sprinkle flour on pastry board and use a floured rolling pin to roll out each half of dough, until it is ⅛ inch thick, or even thinner. It will be a little stiff and hard to roll out, so stop to rest if you need to. Cut out circles with a round cookie cutter or drinking glass and arrange them on baking sheets. Bake about 8 minutes until cookies begin to brown a tiny bit. Remove from oven and baking sheets, and cool on wire rack.
Makes about 5 or 6 dozen.

Switzerland

DELICIOUS LITTLE COOKIES
LECKERLI

(LEH-kehr-lee)

Leckerli is a traditional cookie made the year round in Switzerland. There are many different ways to make *Leckerli*. Sometimes it is made with honey, and sometimes with marzipan (which means it contains ground almonds). It usually is shaped in little molds that leave nice designs on the cookies. Nowadays many Swiss people buy *Leckerli* already made, particularly the *Leckerli* from Basle, which is the best known honey type *Leckerli* and is exported to many parts of the world. The *Leckerli* recipe here is a marzipan type that is a specialty of the confectioners of Zurich. *These cookies have to stand for 24 hours before you bake them.*

INGREDIENTS:

For the cookies:
½ cup ground almonds
   (see page 21)
½ cup confectioners' sugar
1 egg
1 teaspoon lemon juice
½ cup confectioners' sugar

For the icing:
½ cup confectioners' sugar
1 egg white
1 tablespoon lemon juice

UTENSILS: *For the first day: baking sheet, measuring cups and spoons, double boiler, waxed paper, small bowl, cooking spoons, small sharp knife, juice squeezer, table fork or wire whisk, sifter, pizza cutter or plain pastry wheel or small sharp knife, spatula. For the second day: cup, small bowl, egg beater or wire whisk, sifter, measuring cups, cooking spoon, small sharp knife, juice squeezer, spatula or pancake turner, wire rack, pastry brush.*

METHOD: Shaped cookies (see page 13).

Grease and flour baking sheet. Put ground almonds in the top of a double boiler. Sift the ½ cup confectioners' sugar onto a piece of waxed paper, and add to the almonds. Toss together.

Separate an egg, put the yolk in a small bowl, and set aside. Add the unbeaten egg white to the almond mixture, mix well with a spoon, and put in top of double boiler. Put ½ inch of water in the bottom of double boiler and place over medium heat. Bring to boil, and turn to very low. Put the top of the double boiler over the bottom and cook, stirring all the while, until the mixture becomes very thick. This will take almost 10 minutes. Remove from heat.

Squeeze the lemon juice and add it to the almond mixture. Beat the egg yolk lightly with a fork or wire whisk and stir it into the almond mixture. Sift the ½ cup confectioners' sugar onto pastry board. Spoon the almond mixture onto it. Use more confectioners' sugar to coat your fingers, and pat out the almond mixture until it is about ¼ inch thick. Keep sugaring your hands so they won't get sticky. With pizza cutter, pastry wheel, or small sharp knife, cut the almond mixture into small squares about 1-inch square. Dip the spatula into confectioners' sugar and use to transfer squares to the baking sheet. Put the baking sheet in a safe place where it can remain uncovered at room temperature for 24 hours.

After 24 hours, **preheat the oven at 350°.** Bake 10 to 12 minutes until lightly browned.

While *Leckerli* are baking, make the icing. Separate an egg. Put the yolk in a cup and save for another use. Put the white in a small bowl and beat just enough to break up the white and make it a little foamy. Sift confectioners' sugar over egg white and stir in. Squeeze lemon juice and stir in.

When *Leckerli* are done remove from oven, baking sheet, and place on wire rack. With pastry brush apply icing while cookies are hot. Keep cookies on wire rack until icing hardens. **Makes 2 to 2½ dozen.**

Wales

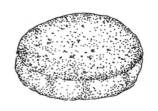

GIRDLE SCONES
CACEN-GRI
(KA-ken GRIH)

Cacen-Gri are baked on a griddle, which is called a "girdle" in Wales and throughout the British Isles. Small flat cakes of this type are often called "scones," pronounced "skahns." They're not too sweet so they can be eaten at any time of the day, including breakfast. You can make them and have them hot with butter, or you can let them cool and put them in the toaster before you eat them.

INGREDIENTS:

1½ cups flour	3 tablespoons sugar
1 teaspoon baking soda	6 tablespoons butter or
1 teaspoon cream of tartar	margarine
pinch of salt	⅔ cup buttermilk

UTENSILS: mixing bowl, sifter, measuring cups and spoons, table knife, pastry blender, cooking spoon, griddle or very heavy frying pan, pastry board, rolling pin, 3-inch round cookie cutter, pancake turner.

METHOD: Griddle cakes (see page 15).

Sift together the flour, baking soda, cream of tartar, salt, and sugar into a mixing bowl. Cut the butter into small pieces and put it with the flour mixture. Cut in the butter with a pastry blender, or use your fingers to rub and work the ingredients together until well blended. Add the buttermilk and mix with a spoon.

Place griddle or frying pan over a very low flame on the stove. Don't grease the griddle.

Sprinkle a little flour on a pastry board and roll out the

dough with a floured rolling pin, until it is ¼ to ½ inch thick. Cut out circles with a round cookie cutter. Using a pancake turner arrange the scones on the hot griddle, cooking about 5 or 6 at a time. Leave some room between each one. Let them cook about 4 or 5 minutes until nicely browned. Turn them with pancake turner and let them brown 4 or 5 minutes on the other side.

Makes about 15.

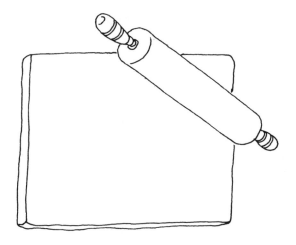

Albania

NUT CAKES
KARIDOPETA

(kah-reh-THO-peh-tah)

Foreign invaders in bygone days and neighboring countries in present times have left their mark on Albanian life. For instance, a great number of words in the Albanian language are of Turkish, Greek, and Slavic origin; and Albanian cooking has been very much influenced by her Greek and Yugoslavian neighbors. *Karidopeta* was originally a Greek pastry and has been adopted by the Albanians.

INGREDIENTS:

For the syrup:
1 cup sugar
½ cup water
½ cup honey
½ teaspoon cinnamon

For the cookies:
½ cup (1 stick) butter or
margarine

½ cup sugar
3 eggs
1 cup very finely chopped
walnuts (see page 21)
½ cup flour
½ teaspoon baking powder
½ teaspoon cinnamon

UTENSILS: saucepan, measuring cups and spoons, cooking spoons, 8-inch by 8-inch baking pan, mixing bowl, waxed paper, sifter, rubber spatula, cake tester, wire rack, small sharp knife, spatula.

METHOD: Bar cookies (see page 14).

The syrup: In a saucepan combine the 1 cup sugar, water, honey, and ½ teaspoon cinnamon. Place over medium heat and cook, stirring constantly, until mixture begins to boil. Turn heat to low and simmer 10 minutes, stirring now and then. Remove from heat and set aside to cool.

The cake: **Preheat oven at 375°.** Butter an 8-inch by 8-inch baking pan. In a mixing bowl cream the butter or margarine until soft. Add the ½ cup sugar and mix well. Add the eggs, one at a time, and mix well each time. Add the walnuts and mix. Onto a piece of waxed paper sift together the flour, baking powder, and ½ teaspoon cinnamon. Add to the dough and mix well.

Scrape the dough out of the bowl into the baking pan and spread out evenly with a rubber spatula. Bake about 25 minutes until lightly browned, and a cake tester inserted in center comes out clean. Remove from oven and set pan on wire rack.

With a small sharp knife cut the cake like this. Then pour the cooled syrup over the hot cake and leave in the pan until completely cool. Remove the pieces with a spatula.
Makes 24.

Bulgaria

YOGURT-NUT COOKIES
MÀZNI KURABÌ

(MAHZ-nee koo-rah-BEE)

Yogurt is a milk culture that looks something like junket dessert. Bulgaria's high-grade milk produces a superior yogurt which is renowned as the best in the world. The Bulgarians are very fond of yogurt and eat it every day, not only because they enjoy it but also because they believe it promotes good health and long life. Yogurt can be eaten plain or it can be mixed with honey or fresh fruit. It is also good in soups, vegetable dishes, salads, breads, and cookies.

INGREDIENTS:

½ cup plain yogurt
½ cup vegetable oil
⅔ cup sugar
½ teaspoon baking soda
1 egg yolk

¾ cup ground walnuts
*   (see page 21)*
2¼ cups flour
¼ cup confectioners' sugar

UTENSILS: mixing bowl, measuring cups and spoons, cooking spoons, cup, waxed paper, sifter, baking sheets, spatula or pancake turner, wire rack, sieve.

METHOD: Shaped cookies (see page 13).

Preheat oven at 350°. Put the yogurt in a mixing bowl and stir until smooth. Gradually add the vegetable oil and stir well each time. Add the ⅔ cup sugar and the baking soda and mix.

Separate an egg. Put the egg white in a cup and save for another use. Add the egg yolk to the yogurt mixture and mix well. Add the walnuts and mix well. Sift the flour onto a piece of waxed paper. Gradually add to the yogurt mixture and mix well. Take small amounts of the dough, about a heaping teaspoonful at a time, and roll into a ball between the palms of your hands. Arrange the balls on ungreased baking sheets. Flatten them a little with the palm of your hand.

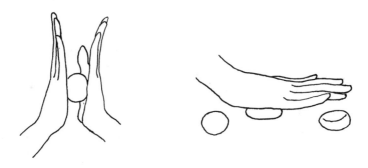

Bake about 20 minutes until lightly browned. Remove from oven and baking sheets, and cool on wire rack. When cookies are cool put confectioners' sugar in a sieve and sift it all over the cookies.
Makes about 3½ dozen.

Czechoslovakia

NUTROLL COOKIES
KOLÁČE
(koh-LAH-chee)

Koláče is made by Czechoslovakian people for Easter and Christmas, and also for festive occasions such as weddings. These cookies are miniature versions of the large *Koláče*, a sweet bread somewhat like a coffee cake, filled with either a walnut or poppyseed mixture, and baked in a long roll or horseshoe shape. The recipe makes a lot of cookies, so it might be fun to share the baking, and the cookies, with a friend.

INGREDIENTS:

For the filling:
2 cups walnuts
2 tablespoons sugar
⅓ cup milk
1 tablespoon honey

For the cookies:
¼ cup milk
1 package active dry yeast
½ cup (1 stick) butter or
    margarine

2 tablespoons sugar
½ teaspoon salt
2 eggs
½ cup sour cream
1 teaspoon vanilla extract
3 cups flour

For the top:
1 egg
1 tablespoon milk

UTENSILS: *meat grinder, measuring cups and spoons, 3 small saucepans, wooden spoons, large bowl, 2 small bowls, egg beater or wire whisk, waxed paper, sifter, baking sheets, rolling pin, pastry board, pizza cutter or small sharp knife, ruler, cup, pastry brush, spatula or pancake turner, wire rack.*

METHOD: Roll and cut cookies (see page 14).

The filling: Grind the walnuts in a meat grinder using a medium blade, or if you have an adult to help you, you can put the walnuts through a blender until they're ground. Place the ground walnuts in a small saucepan with the sugar and milk. Heat over a low flame until the mixture boils, then simmer 5 minutes, stirring all the while. Remove from heat and stir in honey. Allow to cool while you prepare the cookie dough.

The cookies: In a small saucepan heat the milk over a low flame until warm, but not hot. Test milk by putting a drop on your wrist. It should feel warm but not hot enough to burn you. Pour the milk into a large bowl. Sprinkle in the yeast and stir with a wooden spoon until the yeast is dissolved.

In small saucepan melt the butter and add to the yeast mixture. Stir in the sugar and salt.

In small bowl beat eggs lightly with an egg beater or wire whisk and add to yeast mixture. Stir in the sour cream and vanilla extract.

Onto a piece of waxed paper sift the flour. Measure and sift again. Add to the yeast mixture and mix well. Turn out on a pastry board sprinkled with flour. Knead the dough for about 3 minutes. Divide dough into 4 equal parts and allow them to rest on the pastry board for 10 minutes.

Preheat oven at 350°. Grease baking sheets. Roll out one part of dough at a time on a lightly floured pastry board, using a floured rolling pin. Roll dough out as thin as you can— about ⅛ inch thick. With pizza cutter or small sharp knife cut the dough into 2½-inch squares. Use a ruler to help you measure.

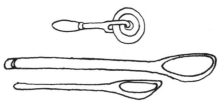

Put about ½ teaspoon of the walnut filling in the center of each square. Fold 1 side over like this. Put some water in a cup to dip your finger into, and moisten the dough here. Then fold over the other side of the dough and pinch the dough together. Arrange filled cookies on baking sheets.

The top: In a small bowl beat 1 egg lightly, and mix in 1 tablespoon milk. With a pastry brush spread some of the egg mixture over each cookie.

Bake 13 to 15 minutes until cookies are golden brown. Remove from oven and baking sheets, and cool on wire rack. Continue rolling out each part of dough and making cookies until dough is used up. If you don't have enough filling for all the cookies you can fill the last ones with any kind of thick jam.

Makes about 10 dozen.

Greece

CLOVE COOKIES
KOURABIEDES

(koo-ram-pe-A-thees)

The Greeks serve *Kourabiedes* at parties and on almost all their festive occasions, and they give them to their children on their Saints' days. In making *Kourabiedes* they spend a lot of time beating the butter, sometimes as long as an hour, which makes the cookies very light in texture. In Greek slang someone who's considered a softy or a pushover is often referred to as a *Kourabiedes.* You'll notice that there's almond extract in *Kourabiedes,* for almonds and honey are ingredients that Greeks especially love in their sweets. Besides cookies and cakes the Greeks also like "spoon sweets," which are similar to jams, flavored with almond, rose, or grapefruit. The spoon sweets are served to a guest with a little spoon and a cup of strong coffee.

INGREDIENTS:

½ cup (1 stick) sweet butter	½ teaspoon vanilla extract
	¼ teaspoon almond extract
⅓ cup confectioners' sugar	1½ cups flour
1 egg yolk	24 whole cloves
1 teaspoon brandy	¼ cup confectioners' sugar

UTENSILS: *bowl, cooking spoons, sifter, measuring cups and spoons, cup, waxed paper, 2 baking sheets, sieve, wire rack, spatula or pancake turner.*

METHOD: Shaped cookies (see page 13).

Remove butter from refrigerator and allow to sit at room temperature for 30 minutes to soften. Put in a bowl and cream until very soft. Continue beating for at least 10 minutes, and longer if you can—the longer the better.

Preheat oven at 350°. Sift ⅓ cup confectioners' sugar over the butter, and mix until blended. Separate an egg. Put the white in a cup and save for another use. Put the yolk in the butter-sugar mixture and mix well. Add the brandy, vanilla extract, and almond extract.

Sift the flour onto a piece of waxed paper. Gradually add to the butter-sugar mixture, mixing well each time. Divide the dough into 4 equal parts. Make 6 cookies out of each part, rolling the dough into balls between the palms of your hands. Arrange 12 balls on each of the ungreased baking sheets. Stick a whole clove into the top of each cookie.

Bake about 18 minutes until cookies are lightly browned. Remove from oven and baking sheets, and cool on wire rack. Put ¼ cup confectioners' sugar in a sieve, and sift over the cookies.

Makes 2 dozen.

Hungary

EVENING FAIRIES
ESTIKE

(esh-TEE-keh)

Hungarians love to stop for tidbits at their pastry shops, and they also like to have sweets at home, where they bake such things as *Estike*. These cookies are prepared and allowed to sit overnight to dry a little and take on the licoricelike flavor of the anise seeds sprinkled over them. This recipe, like most Hungarian cake and pastry recipes, contains no baking powder, but uses lemon juice instead, which the Hungarians feel gives a lighter texture. Perhaps the cookies were named "evening fairies" because people once thought the fairies came to watch over or nibble on the cookies during the night.

INGREDIENTS:

⅔ *cup flour*

2 *eggs*

¾ *cup sugar*

1 *tablespoon lemon juice*

1 *teaspoon vanilla extract*

⅛ *teaspoon salt*

¼ *teaspoon anise seed*

UTENSILS: measuring cups and spoons, sifter, waxed paper, baking sheets, mixing bowl, egg beater or wire whisk, juice squeezer, small sharp knife, cooking spoon, spatula or pancake turner, wire rack.

METHOD: Drop cookies (see page 13).

Onto a sheet of waxed paper sift flour. Butter and flour baking sheets. Squeeze and measure lemon juice.

Break the eggs into a mixing bowl and beat with egg beater or wire whisk until thick and pale in color. This takes about 5 minutes. Gradually add sugar and continue beating a few minutes with egg beater or whisk. Add lemon juice, vanilla extract, and salt and beat 5 more minutes. Gradually add flour and mix well with spoon.

Drop by teaspoonfuls on baking sheets. Drop 2 or 3 anise seeds on top of each cookie. Put the baking sheets in a safe place where they can stay uncovered overnight.

Next day, **preheat oven at 300°**. Bake 12 minutes until cookies are dry, but not brown. Remove from oven and baking sheets, and cool on wire rack.

Makes about 5 dozen.

Latvia

SOUR CREAM BOWKNOTS
TOKORZVARHITJAS

(TAH-karhz-vahr-hit-yahs)

Typical of the many fried cookies made in Slavic countries are these Latvian bowknots. Ingredients may vary a little to include sour cream or different flavorings, but the idea is basically the same whether the cookie is made in Poland, Lithuania, Bulgaria, or Russia. The cookies are rolled and cut, made into bowknot shapes, fried in deep fat or oil, and sprinkled with confectioners' sugar.

INGREDIENTS:

½ cup confectioners' sugar
½ teaspoon grated lemon
    rind
1 egg
6 tablespoons sour cream

1¼ cups flour
¾ teaspoon baking powder
¼ cup confectioners' sugar
    vegetable oil

UTENSILS: cooking spoon, mixing bowl, egg beater or wire whisk, measuring cups and spoons, waxed paper, sifter, grater, pastry board, rolling pin, pizza cutter or plain pastry wheel or small sharp knife, ruler, flat plate, small sharp knife, wok or deep fryer, skimmer or slotted metal spoon, tongs, paper towels, sieve.

METHOD: Fried cookies (see page 15).

Onto a piece of waxed paper sift confectioners' sugar and measure. Grate the lemon rind onto a piece of waxed paper. Break the egg into a mixing bowl and beat lightly with an egg beater or wire whisk. Add ½ cup confectioners' sugar and mix well with a spoon. Add the lemon rind and sour cream and mix well. Onto a piece of waxed paper sift together the flour and baking powder, and gradually add to the egg mixture. Mix well. If the dough is not dry enough add more flour.

Sprinkle some flour on the pastry board and knead the dough there for a few minutes until it is quite elastic. Sprinkle more flour on the pastry board and roll out the dough with a floured rolling pin until it is ⅛ inch thick, or even a little thinner. Cut the dough into strips ¾ inch wide, using a pizza cutter, pastry wheel, or small sharp knife. Then cut diagonally in the opposite direction every 2 inches. Use a ruler to help you measure. The dough will look like this.

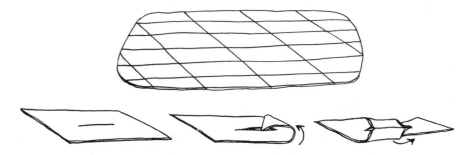

With a small sharp knife cut a slit in each piece of dough. Pick up a piece of dough and pull one end through the slit to form a bowknot. Form all the bowknots and set them on a large plate.

Ask an adult to help you with the next part of this recipe. In a wok or deep fryer pour vegetable oil to a depth of 1½ inches. Heat over medium heat until hot, but not smoking, until you can see little movements on the surface of the oil. With a skimmer or slotted spoon lower about 5 of the bowknots at a time into the hot oil. Let them brown on one side, which will take about 10 seconds. Turn them with tongs and let the other side brown. Remove them with tongs and put on paper towels to drain. Continue until all bowknots have been fried and drained. Turn off stove but do not remove the fryer or wok until it is completely cool.

Put the ¼ cup confectioners' sugar in a sieve and sift over the cookies.

Makes about 5 dozen.

Poland

EASTER CAKES
MAZUREK WIELKANOCNY

(ma-SOO-rek weel-ka-NOE-k'nee)

The most well-known pastry shop in Warsaw, Poland, is Blikle, and it is more than a hundred years old. There one can buy all kinds of luscious pastries and breads all year round, and at holiday times the treats are even more special. At Easter time there is *Mazurek Wielkanocny* and *Babka*, a yeast cake with raisins. On Shrove Tuesday and New Year's Eve people form long lines at the bakery to pick up freshly made *Pączki*, jam-filled doughnuts dear to the hearts of Poles.

INGREDIENTS:

1 cup (2 sticks) butter or	*2 cups confectioners' sugar*
1 stick butter and	*1 teaspoon vanilla extract*
1 stick margarine	*1 egg*
4 eggs	*1 cup thinly sliced almonds* *
2 cups flour	

UTENSILS: saucepan with cover, long-handled spoon, wooden spoons, 2 bowls, small sharp knife, fine sieve, pastry board, plate or waxed paper, 10-inch by 14-inch baking sheet, table knife, sifter, measuring cups and spoons, plastic wrap or waxed paper, rolling pin, small bowl, egg beater or wire whisk, pastry brush, pizza cutter or plain pastry wheel or small sharp knife, spatula or pancake turner, wire rack.

METHOD: Bar cookies (see page 14).

Remove butter from refrigerator and leave at room temperature. Fill a medium-sized saucepan about three-quarters of the way with water. Cover and bring to boil. Remove cover,

* Buy the almonds already sliced or slivered. It's too difficult to slice them yourself.

and with a spoon gently lower 4 eggs into the water, 1 at a time. Boil 12 minutes. Remove pan from stove. Pour boiling water in the sink and fill pan with cold water, covering eggs. When eggs are cool enough to handle, crack and remove shells. Cut eggs in half, and remove yolks. Put the yolks in a fine sieve and push them through with a wooden spoon onto a plate or piece of waxed paper.

Sprinkle a pastry board with flour. Set baking sheet on the flour and trace around it with a table knife. Remove the baking sheet, but don't disturb the flour. Butter the baking sheet very heavily. Flour it very well and knock off the extra flour.

Into a mixing bowl sift together flour and confectioners' sugar. Add sieved yolks, and toss together with a spoon. Cut butter into small pieces and add. With your hands mix and rub ingredients together until well blended. Add vanilla extract and mix again. Push dough into a ball, and wrap in plastic wrap or waxed paper. Put in freezer for 10 minutes.

Preheat oven at 375°. Remove dough from freezer and flatten down with your hands. Place dough on the rectangle you have marked in the flour. Roll out with floured rolling pin so that the dough almost fills the space you have marked. Use your hands to shape the dough and fill in empty spaces. Then starting at the shorter end, drape the dough over the rolling pin, and roll it up loosely around the rolling pin. Transfer it to the baking sheet, and unroll it. Reshape with your fingers so the dough fills the baking sheet and is even all over.

In a small bowl beat 1 egg lightly. With a pastry brush spread the beaten egg over the dough. Sprinkle the sliced almonds over the top. Press the almonds down gently with your hands. Bake about 20 minutes until golden brown. Remove from oven and set baking sheet on the pastry board. Cut lengthwise into 1-inch wide strips. Then cut the opposite way so the pieces are 2 inches long. With a spatula or pancake turner transfer the cookies to a wire rack to cool.
Makes about 6 dozen.

Russia

MINT COOKIES
MIATNIYE PRIANIKI
(mee-YAHT-nee-yeh pree-AH-nee-kee)

This is a very old Russian cookie recipe, a favorite of Madame Alexandra Tolstoy, the daughter of the nineteenth-century Russian Count Leo Tolstoy who wrote such famous books as *War and Peace* and *Anna Karenina*. Madame Tolstoy, who lives in this country and is now over ninety years old, remembers making these mint cookies as a young girl in Russia when all cooking and baking was done on wood-burning stoves. Mint is not used often in Russian cooking, so these cookies were considered quite special (as they still are) and were usually made only at Christmas time. When holiday guests arrived the table kettle, or *samovar*, would be heated with glowing charcoal to make boiling water, and the mint cookies would be served with a pot of fragrant hot tea. Sometimes little paper baskets filled with the cookies would be hung on the Christmas tree.

INGREDIENTS:

1 cup milk
½ teaspoon ammonium
    carbonate (see
    page 24)
1 cup sugar

1 tablespoon corn oil
8 drops peppermint oil *
3¼ cups flour
    pinch of salt

UTENSILS: *measuring cups and spoons, small saucepan, mixing bowl, cooking spoons, sifter, baking sheets, spatula or pancake turner, wire rack.*

METHOD: Shaped cookies (see page 13).

* You can buy peppermint oil at your drugstore.

Preheat oven at 350°. Grease baking sheets. Heat the milk in a small saucepan just to the boiling point, when little bubbles appear on the surface of the milk. Pour the milk into a mixing bowl, add the ammonium carbonate, and mix well. Add the sugar, corn oil, and peppermint oil and mix well. Sift the flour and salt and add to the milk mixture. Stir until smooth.

With a spoon remove small pieces of dough and roll in floured hands, one at a time, to make small balls 1 inch in diameter. Arrange on greased baking sheets.

Bake 10 to 12 minutes. Do not allow to brown. Remove from oven and baking sheets, and cool on wire rack.

Makes about 3½ dozen.

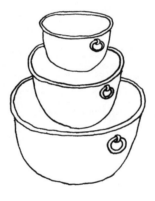

Ukraine

HOLIDAY NUT COOKIES
ROHLICHKY

(roe-LICH-kee)

In the Ukraine there are seemingly endless wheat fields that yield vast amounts of grain for flour. There are also miles and miles of sugar beet fields that produce great amounts of sweetening. This abundance of sugar and flour may be the reason the Ukrainians have developed such a love for baking. They make an infinite variety of cakes, breads, sweet breads, coffee cakes, doughnuts, sticky rolls, tarts, meringues, and cookies. In olden times, cookies such as *Rohlichky* would be heaped on platters along with other sweetmeats and nuts and would be offered to carolers who went from house to house at holiday times singing ancient Ukrainian carols. *Rohlichky* is still made to celebrate holidays in the Ukraine.

INGREDIENTS:
1 cup (2 sticks) butter or
   margarine
½ cup sugar
1 egg white
1 teaspoon vanilla extract

2 cups flour
2 cups ground walnuts,
   hazelnuts, or pecans
   (see page 21)
1 cup confectioners' sugar

UTENSILS: baking sheets, mixing bowl, measuring cups and spoons, cooking spoons, cup, waxed paper, sifter, shallow bowl or soup dish, spatula or pancake turner, wire rack.

METHOD: Shaped cookies (see page 13).

Preheat oven at 375°. Grease baking sheets. Cream the butter or margarine in a mixing bowl until soft. Gradually add

½ cup sugar, mixing well each time. Separate an egg. Put the yolk in a cup and save for another use. Put the unbeaten egg white into the butter-sugar mixture, and mix well. Add vanilla extract.

Onto a piece of waxed paper sift the flour. Gradually add to butter mixture, mixing well each time. Gradually add ground nuts and mix well, either with a spoon or with your hands. Take small pieces of the dough and roll between the palms of your hands to make balls about 1 inch in diameter. Arrange on baking sheets and bake about 12 minutes.

While cookies are baking sift 1 cup confectioners' sugar into a shallow bowl or soup dish. Remove cookies from oven and baking sheets, and roll in the sugar until evenly coated. Set on wire rack to cool.

Makes about 5 dozen.

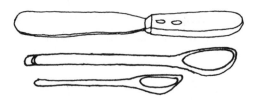

Yugoslavia

WALNUT-FILLED COOKIES
KIFLI

(KEE-flee)

The Yugoslavs serve very hearty food. They like spicy barbe-cued meats, pungent stews, and casseroles laden with vege-tables and meat. Many of their soups are enriched with dumplings or meatballs. Desserts, cakes, and cookies are often heavy, too. Baked goods are usually filled with fruits, like their famous plums—or nuts, like their favorite walnuts. *Kifli* are filled with ground walnuts and are typical of Yugoslav sweets. In summer at sidewalk cafes, people like to eat such pastries with a glass of plum brandy or a cup of thick black coffee.

INGREDIENTS:

The cookies:
½ cup (1 stick) butter or
*   margarine*
2 tablespoons milk
2 tablespoons sour cream
1 package active dry yeast
2 egg yolks
¼ cup sour cream
2 cups flour

The filling:
1 cup finely chopped
*   walnuts (see page 21)*
½ cup sugar
1 teaspoon vanilla extract
2 egg whites

The top:
2 tablespoons milk
¼ cup confectioners' sugar

UTENSILS: measuring spoons and cups, small saucepan, cooking spoons, 2 mixing bowls, small bowl, table knife, plastic wrap or waxed paper, sharp knife with 6- to 8-inch blade or nut chopper, pastry board, egg beater or wire whisk, rubber spatula, baking sheets, rolling pin, ruler, pizza cutter or plain pastry wheel or small sharp knife, cup, pastry brush, spatula or pancake turner, wire rack, sieve.

METHOD: Roll and cut cookies (see page 14).

The cookies: Remove the butter or margarine from the refrigerator and let it sit at room temperature for 30 minutes to soften. Put the milk and 2 tablespoons sour cream in small saucepan and mix until smooth. Place over low heat and heat until just warm, but not hot. You should be able to put a drop of the mixture on the inside of your wrist and have it feel comfortable. Remove from stove and pour into a mixing bowl. Add the package of active dry yeast, and stir until the yeast is completely dissolved. Separate the eggs, and put the egg whites in a small bowl to use later for the filling. Add the yolks, one at a time, to the yeast mixture, and mix well. Stir in the ¼ cup sour cream.

Cut the softened butter into small pieces and add to the dough, mixing until very smooth. Onto a piece of waxed paper sift the flour, and gradually add to the dough. Mix with your hands until the dough is very smooth. Divide the dough into 3 equal parts, and shape each into a ball. Wrap each ball in plastic wrap or waxed paper and put in the refrigerator for 1 hour to chill.

The filling: After the dough has chilled for 30 minutes, chop the walnuts very finely with a large sharp knife on a pastry board, or use a nut chopper. Put them in a mixing bowl, add the sugar, and toss together. Add the vanilla extract and mix. Beat the egg whites you have set aside with an egg beater or wire whisk until soft peaks form. Fold them into the nut mixture with a rubber spatula.

Preheat oven at 350°. Grease baking sheets. Remove dough from refrigerator. Sprinkle a little flour on the pastry board and roll out 1 ball of dough with a floured rolling pin. Keep

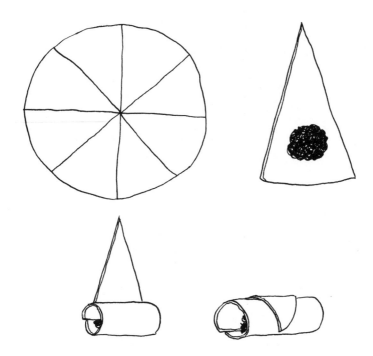

the dough as even in thickness as you can, and roll out a circle about 12 inches in diameter. With a pizza cutter, pastry wheel, or small sharp knife cut the dough into 8 wedges. Put a heaping teaspoon of the filling at the wide part of each wedge. Roll up from wide end to the point, and arrange cookies on baking sheets.

The top: Put the 2 tablespoons milk in a cup and with a pastry brush, brush milk over each cookie. Bake 20 to 25 minutes until golden brown. Remove from oven and baking sheets, and cool on wire rack. Put confectioners' sugar in a sieve and sift over the cookies.

Makes 2 dozen.

Cookies from
Africa and
the Middle East

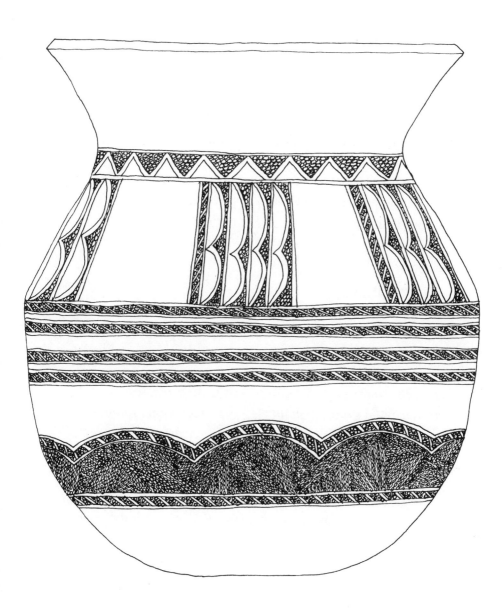

Algeria

ALMOND COOKIES IN SYRUP
MAKROUD EL LOUSE

(MAHK-rood el louse)

Algeria is part of North Africa, an area quite different from the lower part of the African continent. Its people, customs, religion, vegetation, and cooking are more Mediterranean or Middle Eastern. Algerians are fond of Middle Eastern type pastries soaked in sugar syrups. The syrups may be thick or they may be thin and runny, but they are always scented with rose water or orange flower water or sometimes both. Sometimes the pastries are soaked in the syrup, and other times the syrup is just sprinkled on the pastries. A great variety of such pastries are eaten everywhere in North Africa, and *Makroud el Louse* is typical of them.

INGREDIENTS:

For the cookies:
1½ cups ground blanched
     almonds (see pages 20
     and 21)
1½ cups sugar
1 teaspoon grated lemon
     peel
1 egg

2 to 3 tablespoons flour

For the syrup and topping:
½ cup sugar
2 cups water
1 teaspoon orange flower
     water (see page 24)
½ cup confectioners' sugar

UTENSILS: mixing bowl, measuring cups and spoons, meat grinder, grater, waxed paper, cooking spoons, sharp knife, sifter, pancake turner, baking sheets, wire rack, pastry brush, saucepan, flat soup dish, sieve, paper towels.

METHOD: Shaped cookies (see page 13).

Preheat oven at 350°. Put the ground almonds and sugar in a mixing bowl and toss them together. Grate the lemon peel onto a piece of waxed paper, and add to the nuts and sugar. With a spoon make a hole in the center of the mixture to form a well. Break the egg and put it in the well. Mix the ingredients together, starting in the center, until everything is well blended. Press together into a ball.

Sprinkle a little flour on a pastry board and put the ball on it. Roll and press it with your hands to form a roll about 1½ inches thick (*1*). Flatten it down with your hands a little (*2*). Hold a sharp knife slanted and cut the dough into slices about ¾ inch thick (*3*). Lay out the slices and sift the 2 or 3 tablespoons flour over them. Transfer with a spatula or pancake turner to ungreased baking sheets.

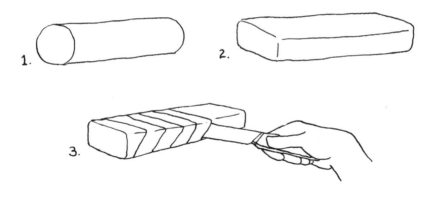

Bake about 12 minutes or until very pale gold. Remove from oven and baking sheets, and cool on wire rack. With pastry brush, brush the flour off the cookies.

While the cookies are baking make the syrup. In a saucepan combine the sugar and water. Bring to a boil, stirring constantly. Lower heat to medium and boil 10 minutes without stirring. Remove from heat and pour syrup into a flat soup dish. Stir in the orange flower water. Allow to cool.

When the cookies and the syrup are both cold, dip the

cookies very quickly into the syrup one at a time. Put them upside down on a wire rack. Put the confectioners' sugar in a sieve, and sift some of it over the cookies. Turn them right side up and set them on paper towels. Sift the rest of the confectioners' sugar over them, using more sugar if you need it. Let the cookies drain on the paper towels for at least 30 minutes before you eat them.

Makes 1 to 1½ dozen.

Congo

COCONUT MACAROONS
MISSIKITI

(miss-i-KEE-tee)

The Congo is a hot, humid country in west-central Africa. The Congolese people grow yams, corn, cassava (from which tapioca is made), rice, peas, bananas, and beans as their most important food crops, and they use fresh coconuts to give many of their main dishes extra flavor. They also make many sweet coconut things that we are familiar with in this country, including coconut fudge, coconut desserts, and the coconut macaroons in this recipe.

INGREDIENTS:

2 egg whites

¾ cup superfine sugar

2 cups flaked coconut

confectioners' sugar

sugar

UTENSILS: baking sheets, cup, mixing bowl, egg beater or wire whisk, measuring cups, cooking spoon, spatula or pancake turner, wire rack.

METHOD: Shaped cookies (see page 13).

Preheat oven at 325°. Grease baking sheets. Separate 2 eggs. Put the yolks in a cup and save for another use. Put the whites in a mixing bowl and beat them with an egg beater or whisk until they form soft peaks when you lift the beater. Don't beat them until they are stiff.

Gradually add the superfine sugar, beating each time. With a spoon mix in the coconut. Dust your hands with confectioners' sugar. Take a small piece of dough and roll between the palms of your hands to make a ball about 1 inch in diameter.

Continue shaping balls until the dough has been used up. Arrange balls on baking sheets. With your fingers sprinkle a little sugar over each cookie.

Bake 16 to 18 minutes until lightly browned. Don't bake the cookies too long, because they should still be soft on the inside. Remove from oven and baking sheets, and cool on wire rack.

Makes about 2½ dozen.

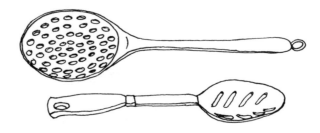

Ethiopia

SPICY BITS
CHIKO
(CHEE-koh)

Ethiopians love spicy foods, so they blend many spices to make a very peppery seasoning they call *berberé*. They use this seasoning in nearly everything they eat. Some of the spices in *berberé* are red pepper, paprika, ginger, cloves, cardamom, coriander, allspice, and fenugreek. *Chiko* also contains many of these spices. You can buy most of them already ground in supermarkets and grocery stores, but you may have to look for fenugreek in a Greek or Middle Eastern food store or in a specialty food store. Ethiopians would use a whole teaspoon of red pepper, or cayenne, in *Chiko*, but we use less in our recipe because most of us are not used to eating such very spicy foods. If you want to make *Chiko* more authentic, just add more red pepper.

INGREDIENTS:

6 tablespoons butter or margarine
1 rounded cup barley flour (see page 24)
½ teaspoon salt
¼ teaspoon ground cloves
¼ teaspoon ground fenugreek
¼ teaspoon ground allspice
½ teaspoon ground cardamom
½ teaspoon ground ginger
¼ teaspoon cayenne or red pepper

UTENSILS: measuring cups and spoons, cooking spoons, small bowl, 1-cup crock or covered glass jar, table knife.

METHOD: Shaped cookies (see page 13).

In a saucepan melt the butter or margarine over low heat. Remove from heat as soon as melted. In a small bowl combine salt, cloves, fenugreek, allspice, cardamom, ginger, and cayenne. Add the melted butter and mix well. Add the barley flour gradually and mix well. Spoon the mixture into a crock or glass jar, and pack it down tightly. Allow to cool.

Put a tight-fitting lid on the crock or jar and put it in the refrigerator. To eat *Chiko*, cut off a little piece and have it any time. Ethiopians eat *Chiko* for breakfast or later in the day with tea, or coffee, or even cocktails.

Makes about 1 cup.

Ghana

SUGAR BREAD
ASIKYIRE PAANO

(ah-SEE-chih-ree PAH-noh)

"Hooting at Hunger" is the name of a harvest festival in Ghana, celebrated joyously in remembrance of the time when the Ga tribe migrated to the coast of Ghana and planted its first crop of Indian corn. Ghanaians celebrate the holiday by wearing gay costumes and feasting mostly on *kpekple,* a corn farina served with a fish and palm nut stew. Corn is one of the Ghanaians' most important staples, and the people depend on it for their daily food as we depend on our wheat and potatoes. These cookies are one example of the many different ways corn is prepared in Ghana.

INGREDIENTS:

1 cup cornmeal (stone-
*   ground if possible)*
2 eggs
½ cup (1 stick) butter or
*   margarine*
1½ cups flour

½ teaspoon salt
½ cup sugar
½ teaspoon nutmeg
1 teaspoon grated lemon
*   rind*

UTENSILS: baking sheets, wooden spoon or wooden spatula, mixing bowl, grater, waxed paper, egg beater or wire whisk, measuring cups and spoons, cooking spoon, table knife, sifter, spatula or pancake turner, wire rack.

METHOD: Shaped cookies (see page 13).

Preheat oven at 300°. Spread the cornmeal on ungreased baking sheets and put in the oven for 20 minutes. Every 4 to 5 minutes stir cornmeal around with a wooden spoon or spatula. Remove from oven.

Grate the lemon rind onto a piece of waxed paper. Grease the baking sheets.

Break the eggs into a mixing bowl and beat lightly with egg beater or wire whisk. Stir in the cornmeal. Cut the butter into small pieces and add to the cornmeal mixture. Mix with your hands until smooth and even.

Onto a piece of waxed paper sift together the flour, salt, sugar, and nutmeg. Add to the cornmeal mixture and mix well with your hands. Add the lemon rind and mix well.

Form the dough into 1-inch balls between the palms of your hands, shaping and patting it together. Arrange balls on baking sheets and flatten with the palm of your hand. Bake 15 minutes. Remove from oven and baking sheets, and cool on wire rack.

Makes 2½ to 3 dozen.

Kenya, Uganda, and Tanzania

FRIED COOKIES
MAANDAZI

(mahn-DAH-zee)

Most people who live in Kenya, Uganda, and Tanzania cook very simply and without modern stoves or ovens. Their diets are generally bland, with corn, rice, bananas, millet, coconut, and yams as the staple foods. Because Arab and Indian immigrants brought spices with them when they settled in this part of the African continent, some people now use a little curry or spice in their cooking. But they have very little meat or sweets, and do almost no baking. When they do have cookies, such as *Maandazi*, for a special occasion, they fry them. *Maandazi* in Swahili, one of the African languages, means simply "pastry."

INGREDIENTS:

1 cup flour	1 egg
1½ teaspoons baking powder	¼ cup water
2 tablespoons sugar	vegetable oil
pinch of salt	

UTENSILS: measuring cups and spoons, sifter, mixing bowl, small bowl, egg beater or wire whisk, plastic wrap, rubber spatula, pastry board, pizza cutter or pastry wheel or small sharp knife, wok or deep fryer, skimmer or slotted metal spoon, tongs, paper towels.

METHOD: Fried cookies (see page 15).

Sift together the flour, baking powder, sugar, and salt into a mixing bowl. In a small bowl beat the egg, add the water, and beat again. Add the egg mixture to the flour mixture and mix well. Knead the dough in the bowl for a few minutes. Cover the bowl with a piece of plastic wrap and let it stand in a warm place for 30 minutes.

Sprinkle some flour on a pastry board, and with a rubber spatula scrape the dough out of the bowl onto the flour. Sprinkle a little more flour over the top of the dough, and pat the dough out with your hands until it is a little more than ¼ inch thick. Cut into 1½-inch squares with a pizza cutter, pastry wheel, or small sharp pointed knife.

Ask an adult to help you with the next part of this recipe. In a wok or deep fryer pour vegetable oil to a depth of 1½ inches. Heat over medium heat until hot, but not smoking, until you can see little movements on the surface of the oil. With a skimmer or slotted spoon lower the dough squares, 2 or 3 at a time, into the hot oil. When they puff up and begin to brown at the edges, turn them over with tongs. When the squares are lightly browned on both sides remove them with tongs and put on paper towels to drain. Continue until all dough squares have been fried and drained. Turn off stove, but do not remove wok or deep fryer until completely cool. **Makes about 1½ dozen.**

Nigeria
PEANUT COOKIES
KULIKULI

(KOO-lee-KOO-lee)

In Nigeria and other parts of West Africa most people eat only one or two meals a day. During the rest of the day they may stop at a snack shop or buy tidbits from a street vendor. Peanut cookies make a good snack here just as they do in their native land, where most cookie recipes contain either locally grown peanuts, cashew nuts, or coconut.

INGREDIENTS:

½ *cup shelled peanuts*
¼ *cup (half a stick) butter*
  or margarine
⅔ *cup sugar*
1 *egg*

1 *teaspoon vanilla extract*
1¼ *cups flour*
½ *teaspoon salt*
½ *teaspoon baking powder*

UTENSILS: *mixing bowl, pastry board, rolling pin, measuring cups and spoons, cooking spoons, waxed paper, sifter, baking sheets, round cookie cutter, spatula or pancake turner, wire rack.*

METHOD: Roll and cut cookies (see page 14).

In a mixing bowl cream the butter until soft. Gradually add the sugar. Add the egg and vanilla extract, and mix well. Onto a piece of waxed paper sift together the flour, salt, and baking powder. Gradually add to the butter mixture, mixing well each time. Place bowl in refrigerator 1 hour to chill. With a rolling pin crush the peanuts on a pastry board.

Preheat oven at 350°. Grease the baking sheets. Spread the crushed peanuts out evenly on the pastry board. Form the chilled dough into a ball and place it on the nuts. Sprinkle a little flour on top of the dough. Press the dough down with your hands to flatten it. Then roll it out about ¼ inch thick with a floured rolling pin. Let the dough cover the nuts as you roll it out.

With a round cookie cutter dipped in flour, cut out as many cookies as you can. Transfer to baking sheets with a spatula or pancake turner. Roll out any leftover dough and cut more cookies. Sprinkle any remaining peanuts over the cookies.

Bake 12 to 15 minutes. Remove from oven and baking sheets, and cool on wire rack.

Makes about 1½ dozen.

Sierra Leone

PEANUT BARS
KANYA
(KAHN-yah)

For about a penny you can buy a bar of *Kanya* from a street vendor in most cities and towns in Sierra Leone. This peanut bar is probably the most popular sweetmeat made throughout West Africa. In some places it's called *Kanya*, in others *Kayan* or *Kanyan*, but it's always made with peanuts or peanut butter. It's very easy to make and requires no cooking.

INGREDIENTS:
½ cup smooth peanut butter   *⅔ cup Cream of Rice*
½ cup superfine sugar   *(uncooked)*

UTENSILS: measuring cups, bowl and wooden potato masher or mortar and pestle, waxed paper or plastic wrap, 5-inch by 9-inch loaf pan, table knife.

METHOD: Bar cookies (see page 14).

Put the peanut butter and sugar in a bowl or a mortar. Pound the sugar and peanut butter together with a pestle, wooden potato masher, or any club-shaped wooden kitchen utensil. If you don't have any of these utensils you'll have to use a wooden spoon and press the mixture over and over against the sides of the bowl. Add Cream of Rice, a little at a time, and continue pounding each time.

Turn the mixture into the loaf pan and press it down evenly with your fingers. Cover the pan with waxed paper or plastic wrap and put in the refrigerator 2 or 3 hours until firm. With a table knife cut into small bars, and lift out with the knife. **Makes 20.**

Tunisia

FLAKY NUT TRIANGLES
SAMSA

(SAHM-sah)

In Tunisia and other parts of North Africa, as well as the Middle East and parts of Europe, a special paper-thin dough is used, layer upon layer, to make delicious flaky pastries in all kinds of shapes—diamonds, triangles, squares, cigars, turbans, and even birds' nests. The pastry dough, which the Tunisians call *brik* or *malsouka*, is made into sheets as thin as tissue paper. Turks call it *yufka*, Greeks call it *phyllo* or *filo*, and other Europeans call it *strudel leaves*. In this country the dough is known by its Greek and European names. It's hard for anyone who isn't a professional baker to make the leaves, but you can buy them here in Middle Eastern groceries, specialty food stores, and some supermarkets already made and frozen. In *Samsa* we use a combination of ground nuts for our filling.

INGREDIENTS:

1 2-ounce box phyllo pastry dough

3 tablespoons ground almonds (see page 21)

3 tablespoons ground walnuts

3 tablespoons ground pistachios

3 tablespoons ground pine nuts

¼ cup sugar

¼ cup (half a stick) butter

½ cup honey

UTENSILS: *clean dish towel, meat grinder, small bowl, measuring cups and spoons, cooking spoons, 2 small saucepans, pastry brush, 2 baking sheets, small sharp knife, ruler, small spoon, spatula or pancake turner, wire rack, serving plate.*

METHOD: Shaped cookies (see page 13).

If the phyllo pastry is frozen, remove it from the freezer and allow it to thaw completely at room temperature. This will take about 2 hours.

Moisten a dish towel with water, and wring it out very tightly so that the towel is just damp. Unwrap the phyllo pastry and lay it out flat on a pastry board. Put the damp towel over it.

If you aren't able to buy ground nuts, put enough nuts through a meat grinder with a coarse blade to make 3 tablespoons of each kind of ground nut. Then put them through the meat grinder together, using a fine blade. Put the nuts in a small bowl and mix them with the sugar.

Put the butter in a small saucepan and let it melt over low heat. Remove from heat as soon as melted.

Preheat oven at 350°. Grease baking sheets. With a small sharp knife cut straight down through the phyllo leaves to make a row of strips 2 inches wide. The phyllo leaves are about 11 or 12 inches wide, so you will have a layer of strips 2 inches wide and 11 or 12 inches long. Peel off a strip and lay it on the pastry board. Put the damp towel back over the phyllo when you aren't working with it. With a pastry brush spread melted butter over the phyllo strip. Put a heaping teaspoon of the nut filling at the bottom of the strip. Fold the dough over the filling this way. Then keep on folding until

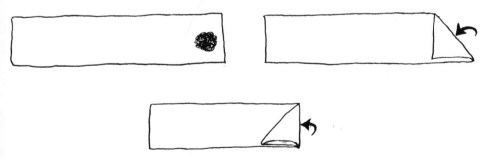

you get to the other end. Put the triangle on the baking sheet, and brush the top of it with melted butter.

Remove another strip of phyllo and make another triangle the same way. Continue until you've made 24 triangles, or until the filling is used up. Cut more 2-inch wide strips of phyllo as you need them.

Bake triangles about 12 minutes until lightly browned. Remove from oven and baking sheets, and cool on wire rack. Arrange on a serving plate.

Heat the honey in a small saucepan over low heat for just 1 or 2 minutes, stirring until it becomes runny. Pour honey over the triangles.

Makes about 2 dozen.

Egypt

PUFFY FRITTERS IN SYRUP
ZALABIA

(zah-LAH-bee-ah)

Zalabia is a fritter popular in Egypt and other Middle Eastern countries. One can buy *Zalabia* in the streets during festival times in Egypt. The dough is often colored red or yellow to express joy and happiness, and the fritters are sprinkled with sugar and sometimes cinnamon. In Lebanon people prefer to dip their *Zalabia* in halvah, a mixture of ground sesame seeds and honey. In some places *Zalabia* is still called by its medieval name, *Luqmat el Qadi*, which means "judge's mouthfuls."

INGREDIENTS:

For the fritters:
1   package active dry yeast
¼   cup warm water
1   teaspoon sugar
1   cup water
1¼ cups milk
3½ cups flour
    vegetable oil

For the syrup:
2½ cups sugar

1¼ cups water
1½ teaspoons lemon juice
1   teaspoon rose water
    (see page 24)
1   teaspoon orange flower
    water (see page 24)

For the top:
¼   cup sugar
½   teaspoon cinnamon

UTENSILS: measuring cups and spoons, cup, cooking spoons, 2 saucepans (1 with a cover), mixing bowl, sifter, clean dish towel, small sharp knife, juice squeezer, heavy saucepan or wok or deep fryer, tongs, paper towels, fork, platter, small bowl.

METHOD: Fried cookies (see page 15).

The fritters: Take ¼ cup of warm water from the hot water faucet and put it in a cup. The water should be very warm, but not hot enough to hurt you if you run it on the inside of your wrist. Sprinkle the package of yeast over the warm water, and stir with a spoon until yeast is dissolved. Add the sugar and stir until dissolved. Put the cup in a warm place, such as the back of the stove, for about 10 minutes until yeast mixture starts to get frothy. While you're waiting, put the 1 cup water and the milk into a saucepan and heat over medium heat until just warm, not hot. Remove from heat and stir the yeast mixture into milk and water.

Sift the flour into the mixing bowl. Pour the yeast mixture into the flour with one hand while you stir with the other. Mix until very smooth. Wet a clean dish towel with hot water and wring it out very well. Cover the bowl with the damp towel and set in a warm place for 1 hour.

The syrup: Squeeze the lemon juice. In a saucepan combine the sugar, water, and lemon juice. Cook over medium heat, stirring all the while, until the mixture boils and the sugar is dissolved. Lower the heat and simmer 5 minutes, stirring occasionally. Remove from heat and stir in the rose water and orange flower water. Allow to cool. Cover with lid and put syrup in refrigerator.

After 1 hour has passed remove the dish towel from the bowl of dough. You'll see that the dough has risen and is very bubbly. Stir the dough until the bubbles are gone. Cover again with the towel, set in a warm place, and leave for 1 more hour.

Ask an adult to help you with the next part of this recipe. Pour oil into a heavy saucepan, wok, or deep fryer until it is about 1½ inches deep. Place on stove and heat over medium heat until hot, but not smoking, until you can see little movements on the surface of the oil. Remove the dish towel from the bowl and stir the dough. Drop the dough into the hot fat by teaspoonfuls, making about 4 fritters at a time. When they are golden brown, turn them over with tongs and let them brown on the other side. Sometimes they turn over by themselves, so make sure they get browned on both sides. Remove fritters with tongs and drain on paper towels.

When all the fritters are finished turn off the stove, but do not dispose of the oil until it has cooled completely. Take the syrup from the refrigerator, and with your fingers or a fork dip each fritter into the syrup. Hold the fritters up so that the extra syrup can drip off, and arrange them on a large platter.

In a small bowl mix together the ¼ cup sugar and the cinnamon. Sprinkle it over the fritters.

Makes about 5 dozen.

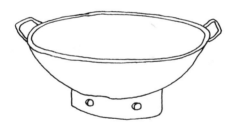

Iran

PERSIAN COOKIES
NANE SHIRINI

(nah-neh shee-REE-nee)

Jams, pastries, puddings, ice cream, fruits, and cookies of all kinds are eaten in great quantities in Iran. Iranians like sweet tastes so much that they sometimes make a rice dish with sugar syrup and serve it with the main part of their meal. The biggest time for sweets is March 21, the first day of spring, when the Iranian New Year begins. Then there are thirteen days of celebrating, with people feasting on mountains of cakes, sweetmeats, and cookies like *Nane Shirini.*

INGREDIENTS:

1 cup (2 sticks) butter or margarine
1 cup sugar
2 egg yolks
1 teaspoon vanilla extract

1 teaspoon almond extract
1 teaspoon lemon juice
2 cups flour
1 teaspoon baking powder

UTENSILS: mixing bowl, measuring cups and spoons, cooking spoons, cup, small sharp knife, juice squeezer, waxed paper, sifter, baking sheets, spatula or pancake turner, wire rack.

METHOD: Shaped cookies (see page 13).

In a mixing bowl cream the butter or margarine until soft. Gradually add the sugar and mix well. Separate 2 eggs. Put the egg whites in a cup and save for another use. Add the egg yolks to the butter-sugar mixture and mix well. Squeeze the lemon juice and add it and the vanilla and almond extracts to the butter mixture.

Onto a piece of waxed paper sift together the flour and

baking powder. Add gradually to the dough, and mix well as you add. Place dough in refrigerator for 30 minutes to chill.

Preheat oven at 325°. Take teaspoonfuls of dough and roll between your hands to form small balls. Arrange the balls on ungreased baking sheets. With your thumb press down on the cookies to flatten them a little. Bake 12 to 15 minutes until lightly browned. Remove from oven and baking sheets, and cool on wire rack.

Makes about 2½ dozen.

Israel

HAMAN'S POCKETS
HAMANTASCHEN

(HAH-mahn-tah-shen)

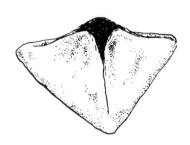

Hamantaschen are the traditional sweets of Purim, the merriest holiday on the Jewish calendar. Purim takes place in the early springtime and celebrates the deliverance of the Jews long ago in Persia from the plotting of the Persian prime minister, Haman. The cookies represent Haman's triangular-shaped pockets, which were filled with silver coins given him to massacre the Jews. These cookies are baked with poppy-seed, prune, or apricot fillings. *Hamantaschen* are also known as "Haman's hats" and "Haman's donkey ears."

INGREDIENTS:

¼ cup vegetable oil
⅓ cup sugar
2 eggs
1 teaspoon vanilla extract
2 cups flour
1 teaspoon baking powder
  pinch of salt

1 10-ounce can or jar poppy-seed filling, lekvar (prune butter), or apricot butter (see page 24)

For the top:
1 egg
1 tablespoon cold water

UTENSILS: *mixing bowl, measuring cups and spoons, cooking spoons, waxed paper, sifter, baking sheets, pastry board, rolling pin, large round cookie cutter 3½ to 4 inches in diameter or a drinking glass of the same size, pancake turner, cup, small bowl, egg beater or wire whisk, pastry brush, wire rack.*

METHOD: Roll and cut cookies (see page 14).

In a mixing bowl combine the vegetable oil and sugar. Add the 2 eggs and mix until well blended. Add the vanilla extract. Onto a piece of waxed paper sift together the flour, baking powder, and salt. Gradually add to the egg mixture, mixing well each time. Put dough in refrigerator to chill for 1 hour, or in the freezer for 15 minutes.

Preheat oven at 350°. Grease baking sheets. Sprinkle some flour on the pastry board and roll out the dough with a floured rolling pin until it is about ⅛ inch thick. Cut out as many circles as you can using a round cookie cutter or the rim of a drinking glass. With the pancake turner transfer 6 circles to a baking sheet. Put a heaping teaspoon of poppyseed filling, lekvar, or apricot butter in the center of each circle.

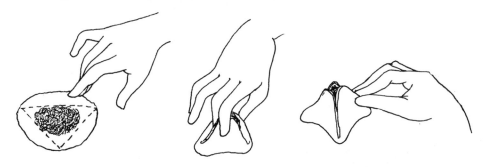

Put a little cold water in a cup and, dipping your finger into it, moisten the edge of a circle.

Then pick up the sides of the circle and bring them up and together to form a triangle, like this. Pinch the edges together so that there is only a tiny space open at the top. Do the same with the rest of the other circles.

In a small bowl beat the egg and the tablespoon of cold water with an egg beater or wire whisk. Brush some of this mixture on each cookie with a pastry brush, coating evenly all over. Bake 18 minutes. Remove from oven and baking sheets, and cool on wire rack.

Makes about 2½ dozen.

Lebanon

SEMOLINA COOKIES
MA'AMOUL

(mah-AH-mool)

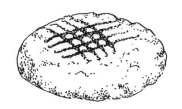

The Lebanese, as well as other people in the Middle East and North Africa, use a great deal of semolina in their cooking. Semolina comes from the protein and starch portion of a very hard wheat called durum wheat. Semolina looks like very fine cornmeal, and is used like flour. (In our own country, macaroni is made from semolina.) When it's formed into tiny granular balls and cooked something like rice, the Lebanese call it *couscous* (pronounced KOOS-koos). They often serve *couscous* with chicken or meat dishes. *Ma'Amoul* contains semolina and two other Middle Eastern favorites, orange flower water and rose water. The Lebanese use these flavorings in their cooking in much the same way that we use vanilla extract.

INGREDIENTS:

½ cup (1 stick) butter
1 cup semolina
1 cup boiling water
  flour
¼ cup finely chopped
  walnuts (see page 21)
2 tablespoons sugar

½ teaspoon orange flower
  water (see page 24)
½ teaspoon rose water (see
  page 24)
2 tablespoons confectioners'
  sugar

UTENSILS: measuring cups and spoons, mixing bowl, teakettle or saucepan, cooking spoons, table knife, plastic wrap or aluminum foil, pastry board, dough scraper or metal spatula, baking sheets, sharp knife with 6- to 8-inch blade or nut chopper, small bowl, little spoon, table fork, spatula or pancake turner, wire rack, sieve.

METHOD: Shaped cookies (see page 13).

Remove butter from refrigerator and allow to stand at room temperature for 30 minutes. Put the semolina in a mixing bowl. Boil some water, measure 1 cupful, and add it to the semolina, mixing well. Cut the butter into small pieces with a table knife and add to the semolina, mixing well until smooth and well blended. Cover the bowl with plastic wrap or aluminum foil and *put in the refrigerator to chill for 6 hours or longer. You can leave it overnight if you want to.*

Remove the chilled semolina mix from the refrigerator and put it on a pastry board. Knead it for about 5 minutes. Use a dough scraper or metal spatula to pick up the dough each time it sticks to the pastry board. Flour your hands and divide the dough into 10 equal parts. Roll each part between your hands to form 10 balls. Set them on the pastry board and with your thumbs push a large hollow in the center of each one, without going all the way through to the bottom.

Preheat oven at 350°. Grease baking sheets. Chop the walnuts and put them in a small bowl. Mix in the 2 tablespoons sugar. Add the orange flower water and rose water, and mix well. With a little spoon fill the hollows in the cookie balls with this mixture.

Flour your hands again and pinch the dough together up and around the filling so that the filling is completely covered. Arrange 5 cookies on each baking sheet, and flatten them a little with the open palm of your hand. With a fork make some crisscross marks on top of each cookie. (In Lebanon the cookies are pressed into wooden molds to make patterns on them.) Bake 25 to 28 minutes. Remove from oven and baking sheets, and cool on wire rack.

While cookies are still warm, sift confectioners' sugar over them.
Makes 10.

Saudi Arabia, Jordan, Iraq
DATE CAKES
TAMRIAH
(tahm-REE-yah)

Dates are more than one-half sugar. They make a marvelous candy-fruit for people living in the Holy Land and North African areas where dates are grown. The cooking of Saudi Arabia, Jordan, and Iraq is very similar, and the people all enjoy making and eating little date cakes such as the ones in this recipe. Even the camels get to enjoy dates, because the date pits are ground up to make feed for them.

INGREDIENTS:

3 tablespoons finely
  chopped walnuts (see
  page 21)
¼ cup flour

½ pound (8 ounces) pitted
  dates
3 tablespoons butter

UTENSILS: cutting board and sharp knife with 6- to 8-inch blade or nut chopper, mixing bowl, measuring cups and spoons, cooking spoons, meat grinder, small saucepan, pastry board, small sharp knife, frying pan, pancake turner.

METHOD: Shaped cookies (see page 13).

Chop the walnuts and place in a mixing bowl with the flour. Toss together.

Put the dates through a meat grinder with a medium blade. Add the ground dates to the nut mixture, and mix well with your hands until well blended.

Put the butter in a small saucepan and place over low heat until melted. Remove from heat. Measure 1 tablespoon of the melted butter and add it to the date mixture. Mix with your hands until well blended. Place the date mixture on a pastry board and roll it back and forth with your hands, shaping it to form a roll about 2 inches in diameter. With a small sharp knife slice the date roll into eight or nine slices.

Lay the slices on the pastry board and flatten them out a little with your hands. Put the rest of the melted butter in a frying pan and add the date slices. Place over a medium low flame and sauté until the slices are just lightly browned, about 2 minutes. With a pancake turner turn them over and brown on the other side for 1 minute or less. Watch carefully as the slices will get dark quickly, and you don't want to burn them. Remove slices with a pancake turner.

You can serve the date cakes as a hot dessert with some heavy cream that's been whipped just enough to hold its shape, or you can let the date cakes cool and eat them like cookies.

Makes 8 or 9.

Syria

RENDERED BUTTER COOKIES
GHORAYBEH

(go-RAY-beh)

Rendered butter is butter that's been melted, simmered, cooled, and strained. It's used for cooking a great deal in Middle Eastern countries where many people don't have refrigerators. Rendered butter doesn't have to be kept cold, and stays fresh a long time. Another name for rendered butter is clarified butter, and in India it's called *ghee*. We're going to make some to use in this cookie recipe for *Ghoraybeh*.

INGREDIENTS:

½ *pound (2 sticks) butter*
1 *tablespoon whole wheat flour or cracked wheat* *
1 *cup sugar*
½ *teaspoon rose water (see page 24) or ¼ teaspoon almond extract*

2 *cups flour*
  confectioners' sugar

UTENSILS: saucepan, measuring cups and spoons, cooking spoons, strainer, cheesecloth, mixing bowl, waxed paper, sifter, baking sheets, spatula or pancake turner, sieve.

METHOD: Shaped cookies (see page 13).

Put the butter in a saucepan and place over medium heat. When the butter has melted and is beginning to bubble, turn the heat as low as you can, and stir in 1 tablespoon whole wheat flour or cracked wheat. Cook on very low flame, un-

---

* You can buy cracked wheat in health food stores or in grocery stores where Middle Eastern or Indian people shop.

covered, for 1 hour. Don't stir at all. Remove mixture from stove and allow to stand for 30 minutes. Line a strainer with 2 layers of cheesecloth, and pour the butter mixture through the strainer into a mixing bowl.

Preheat oven at 300°. Add the sugar and rose water or almond extract to the strained mixture, and mix well. Onto a piece of waxed paper sift the 2 cups flour. Gradually add to the butter mixture, mixing well. Knead the dough with your hands in the bowl for a few minutes.

Pull off small pieces of dough and roll them between the palms of your hands into balls or ovals. Arrange on ungreased baking sheets and flatten slightly with the palm of your hand. Bake 15 minutes.

Remove from oven and allow to cool on baking sheets. Remove from baking sheets and sift the confectioners' sugar over them.

Makes about 3½ dozen.

Cookies from the Far East, Pacific Islands, and Australia

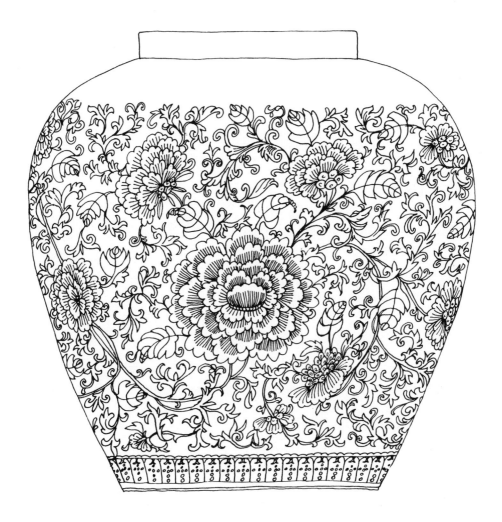

Burma

COCONUT FRITTERS
MOK-SI-KYO
(mawk-see-kyaw)

In Burma a sweet dish is occasionally served in the middle of dinner because the Burmese feel that's a nourishing way to eat. But they generally end their meal with fruit, especially mangoes, and save pastry like *Mok-si-kyo* for snack time. Pastries and sweetmeats are often made with coconut, nuts, and raisins, and some are tinted with food coloring.

INGREDIENTS:

½ cup flour
½ cup rice flour (see
    page 24)
    pinch of salt
    pinch of baking soda
⅓ cup flaked, unsweetened
    coconut

½ cup brown sugar, firmly
    packed
1¼ cups water
    vegetable oil

UTENSILS: mixing bowl, sifter, measuring cups and spoons, cooking spoons, wok or deep fryer, tongs, paper towels.

METHOD: Fried cookies (see page 15).

Into a mixing bowl sift together the flour, rice flour, salt, and baking soda. Add the coconut and brown sugar, and toss together. Add the water and stir until well blended.

    Ask an adult to help you with the next part of this recipe. Pour 1 inch of vegetable oil in a wok or deep fryer and place over medium heat. Heat oil until you can see little movements on the surface of the oil. Make the fritters, 1 at a time, by

dropping 1 tablespoon of the batter into the hot fat. When the fritter browns at the edges, turn it over with tongs. Fry until brown, remove with tongs, and drain on paper towels. Do not let the oil become too hot, or the fritters will fall apart as they cook. Turn the heat down if necessary.
Makes about 2 dozen.

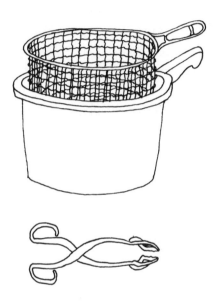

Ceylon

POTATO CAKES
AARDAPPLEN KOEKEN

(AHRD-ahp-plen KOO-kehn)

The people who came from other countries to live in Ceylon have influenced the kind of cooking that is done in Ceylon today. Indian, Dutch, English, and Portuguese cooking have all mingled with native Ceylonese cooking. If you're familiar with the Dutch language you may be able to tell from the name of this recipe that these potato cakes are Dutch in origin. They come from a community in Ceylon where many Dutch people settled. *Aardapplen Koeken*, which are really pancakes, have become as much a part of Ceylonese cuisine as the local curry dishes and great assortment of tropical fruits.

INGREDIENTS:

½ cup flaked, unsweetened coconut
1 cup warm water
2 medium-sized potatoes cold water
1 teaspoon salt

2 eggs
1 cup flour
pinch of salt
¼ cup of sugar
1 tablespoon butter or margarine

UTENSILS: *2 mixing bowls, small bowl, measuring cups and spoons, vegetable brush, potato peeler, sharp knife, saucepan, long-handled fork, colander or sieve, potato masher, fork, wooden spoon, frying pan, pancake turner.*

METHOD: Pancakes (see page 15).

Put the coconut and warm water in a mixing bowl and allow to stand for 20 minutes. Pour the water into a small bowl, and squeeze as much liquid from the coconut as you can with your hands. This liquid is coconut milk. (You can throw away the used coconut.)

While the coconut stands in the water you can prepare the potatoes. Wash and peel potatoes. Cut them into cubes about 1 inch square, until you have 1½ cupfuls. Put them in a saucepan and pour in cold water to about 2 inches above the potatoes. Add the 1 teaspoon salt. Put the saucepan on the stove and cook over high heat until the water boils. Turn the heat down to medium and boil for 10 minutes. Turn off the stove. Take the potatoes out of the water with a long-handled fork and put them in a colander or sieve to drain. Empty the cooking water from the pan and put the drained potatoes back in the pan. Mash them with a potato masher until they are smooth and no lumps are left.

In a mixing bowl beat 1 egg lightly with a fork. Stir in the mashed potatoes with a wooden spoon. Add half of the flour and mix well. Add another egg and mix well. Add the rest of the flour and mix until smooth. Add the coconut milk a little at a time, and mix well each time. Add a pinch of salt and the sugar, and mix.

Put the butter in a frying pan, place over a medium flame, and allow to melt. Spoon in the batter, 1 tablespoon at a time, making 4 cakes at a time. When brown on one side, turn each cake over with a pancake turner and brown the other side. Make more pancakes until the batter is used up, adding more butter if you need it. (If you prefer you can make some pancakes one day, store the remaining batter in a tightly covered glass jar in the refrigerator, and make more pancakes the next day.)

Eat with a fork while cakes are still hot, and serve with butter and brown sugar if you like.

Makes about 2½ dozen.

China

ALMOND COOKIES
HANG GEEN BENG

(hahng geen bee-EHNG)

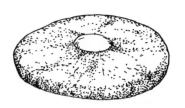

Very few cattle are raised in China, and consequently dairy products such as milk, cheese, and butter are scarce. The Chinese do raise pigs, and lard or pork fat is used instead of butter in Chinese baking. When people say "meat" in China, they mean pork. If you prefer not to use lard you can use vegetable shortening when you make these almond cookies, but they won't taste quite the same.

INGREDIENTS:

2½ cups flour
¼ teaspoon salt
1 teaspoon baking powder
1 cup sugar
1 cup lard or vegetable
   shortening
1 egg

1 teaspoon almond extract
1 tablespoon cold water
4 dozen whole blanched
   almonds (see page 20)
1 egg yolk
1 tablespoon water

UTENSILS: mixing bowl, sifter, measuring cups and spoons, pastry blender, 2 small bowls, egg beater or wire whisk, cooking spoons, baking sheets, cup, pastry brush, spatula or pancake turner, wire rack.

METHOD: Shaped cookies (see page 13).

Into a bowl sift together the flour, salt, baking powder, and sugar. Add the lard or vegetable shortening and cut it in with a pastry blender or rub it between your fingers until it's crumbly.

In a small bowl beat the egg lightly with an egg beater or wire whisk. Add the almond extract. Add this egg mixture to the flour mixture, and toss together. Add the tablespoon of cold water and mix quickly with your hands to form a firm dough. Push dough together into a ball. Put in the refrigerator for 1 hour to chill.

Preheat oven at 350°. Grease baking sheets. Remove dough from refrigerator and shape into 1½-inch balls by rolling pieces of dough between the palms of your hands. Place the balls on baking sheets and flatten them gently with your hand. Press an almond into the center of each cookie.

Separate an egg. Put the white in a cup and save for another use. Put the yolk in a small bowl and mix it with 1 tablespoon of water. Brush some of this mixture over each cookie, using a pastry brush.

Bake about 12 minutes until lightly browned. Remove from oven and baking sheets, and cool on wire rack.
Makes about 4 dozen.

India

SESAME SWEETS
SESAME CHIKKIS

(SEH-sah-meh CHEEK-kees)

There are so many kinds of sweets in India and many take such great time and skill to prepare that professional sweet makers, called *mithai-walas,* are found in a section of almost every city and town, where they have shops in which to make and sell their particular specialties. Some of the simpler sweets, such as the ones in this recipe, are made at home, especially during October and November, a time of many holidays in India. The sweets often play an important part in these holidays. For instance, during *Shraddha,* a holiday honoring the dead, sweets are given to the birds, and when the sweets have been eaten the people feel that the dead have been satisfied and that their own feasting can begin. During the season's biggest festival, *Divali,* the Festival of Lights, people visit one another's homes, exchanging presents and eating many sweets. On the last evening of this four- or five-day holiday, they offer sweets to the goddess Laxmi so that the following year will be a productive one for all.

INGREDIENTS:

½ cup (1 stick) butter
2 teaspoons whole wheat
   flour
1 cup sesame seeds

¼ cup whole wheat flour
½ cup dark brown sugar
2 tablespoons water

UTENSILS: small saucepan, measuring cups and spoons, cooking spoons, small strainer, cheesecloth, cup, frying pan, 2 plates, paper towels, table knife.

METHOD: Shaped cookies (see page 13).

Put the butter in a saucepan and place over medium heat. When the butter has melted and is beginning to bubble, turn the heat as low as you can and stir in the 2 teaspoons whole wheat flour. Cook on a very low flame, uncovered, for 1 hour. Don't stir at all. Remove mixture from stove and allow to stand for 30 minutes. Line a small strainer with 2 layers of cheesecloth, and pour the butter and wheat flour mixture through the strainer into a cup. This is now called rendered butter or *ghee*.

Put the sesame seeds in a frying pan and place over a low flame. Heat them for several minutes, stirring all the time, until they become lightly browned. Don't let them get too brown or they'll burn. Remove them from the heat and turn them onto a plate. Wipe out the pan quickly with a paper towel.

Put 1 tablespoon of the rendered butter in the frying pan and place it over low heat. Stir in the ¼ cup whole wheat flour and stir for 5 minutes, being careful not to let the flour scorch or burn. Remove from the heat and turn onto the plate with the sesame seeds. Again wipe out the pan quickly with a paper towel.

Put the remaining rendered butter in the frying pan, add the brown sugar, and mix well, over low heat. Add the water and continue to stir for a minute or two until the mixture becomes thick. Add the sesame seeds and flour mixture and cook, stirring, over low heat for about 5 minutes, or until the mixture becomes quite thick and sticks together well. Remove from the heat and turn out onto a plate. As soon as the mixture is cool enough to handle, cut it into 10 equal parts. Shape each part with your hands into a ball. Cool completely before eating.
Makes 10.

Korea

CINNAMON FOLDOVERS
MILS-SAM
(meels-sahm)

Most Korean cookies are fried, rather than baked. Many contain pine nuts or hazelnuts, which are Korean favorites. Koreans also love sweetmeats made with chestnuts, raisins, or ginger. For special festivals they make huge round cakes topped with icing characters or letters that spell out greetings such as "long life" or "lots of male children," just as we would ice a cake to say "happy birthday."

INGREDIENTS:

2 tablespoons sesame seeds	*6 tablespoons water*
1 teaspoon cinnamon	*1 tablespoon or more*
1 tablespoon sugar	*vegetable oil*
1 cup flour	*about 14 small celery*
¾ teaspoon salt	*leaves (optional)*
1 teaspoon baking powder	

UTENSILS: measuring spoons and cups, small heavy frying pan, cooking spoons, mortar and pestle, mixing bowl, sifter, pastry board, rolling pin, pizza cutter or plain pastry wheel or small sharp knife, frying pan, tongs, fork, paper towels.

METHOD: Pancakes (see page 15).

Put the sesame seeds in a small heavy frying pan. Place over low heat and stir the seeds until they are light brown. Don't let them get dark. Remove from stove and put them in a mortar. Pound them with a pestle until they are broken down into a paste and you can no longer see any seeds. Add the cinnamon and sugar.

Into a mixing bowl sift together the flour, salt, and baking powder. Add the water all at once and mix well with your hands. If you can't get all the flour mixed into the water, add 1 more tablespoon of water. If the dough is still too dry, add a little more water, but don't let it get too sticky or you won't be able to roll it out.

Sprinkle a little flour on the pastry board and roll out the dough with a floured rolling pin until it is less than ⅛ inch thick. With a pastry wheel, pizza cutter, or small sharp knife, cut the dough into strips 2 inches wide. Then cut the opposite way to make the strips 4 inches long. If the pieces shrink a little pick them up and stretch them with your hands.

Pour a tablespoon of vegetable oil into a frying pan, and heat the oil over a medium flame for about half a minute. Fry 2 dough pieces at a time, on one side only. Don't let them get brown—just heat until you begin to see bubbles form in the dough. Then remove the dough pieces with tongs and lay them, fried side up, on the pastry board. Continue frying the pieces on one side until all are finished and resting on the pastry board. If your frying pan gets dry as you work, add another tablespoon of oil.

Place a small spoonful of the sesame-cinnamon mixture on each piece of fried dough. Then fold it over in the middle as though closing a book. Seal the open edges together by pressing all around them with a fork like this. Lay a small celery leaf on each foldover.

Add another tablespoon of oil to the frying pan, and over medium flame fry the foldovers on one side until brown, then turn over with tongs and fry on the other side until brown. Remove from frying pan with tongs and drain on paper towels, leaf side up. Serve hot or cold.
Makes about 14.

Thailand

COCONUT MILK COOKIES
TONG EK
(TONG eck)

In Thailand, as in many parts of Eastern Asia, the people eat a good deal of fresh fruit instead of cakes and cookies. When they do make cookies or cakes they use ingredients that come from foods that grow in the area, such as coconut milk, rice flour, palm sugar, dates, lotus seeds, mung beans, or cassava root. The Thai people like flower scents in their food, and jasmine syrup is one of their favorites for flavoring cakes and cookies. Sometimes they set a bouquet of fragrant flowers next to their baked goods or burn a jasmine-scented candle nearby so that the scent will transfer to the food.

INGREDIENTS:

½ *cup unsweetened, flaked*
      coconut
½ *cup hot water*
¾ *cup chopped walnuts or*
      other nuts (see page 21)
1½ *cups flour*

1 *teaspoon baking powder*
¾ *cup sugar*
½ *cup (1 stick) butter or*
      margarine
2 *egg yolks*

UTENSILS: 2 small bowls, measuring cups and spoons, sharp knife with 6- to 8-inch blade or nut chopper, baking sheets, mixing bowl, sifter, table knife, pastry blender, small strainer, cups, cooking spoons, egg beater or wire whisk, spatula or pancake turner, wire rack.

METHOD: Drop cookies (see page 13).

In a small bowl combine the coconut and hot water and let stand for 20 minutes.

Preheat oven at 350°. Grease baking sheets. Chop the nuts. Into a mixing bowl sift together the flour, baking powder, and sugar. Cut the butter into small pieces and add to the flour mixture. Cut in with a pastry blender or rub mixture between your fingers until it looks crumbly.

Take the coconut-water mixture and with your hands squeeze the coconut in the water for a few minutes. Then pour the mixture through a small strainer into a cup, squeezing out as much liquid as you can from the coconut. The liquid you have now is coconut milk. (You can throw away the coconut.) Add it to the flour mixture and toss together.

Separate 2 eggs. Put the whites in a cup and save for another use. Put the yolks in a small bowl and beat lightly with an egg beater or wire whisk. Add to the dough and mix well. Add the nuts and mix well.

Drop by teaspoonfuls on baking sheets. Bake about 10 minutes. Remove from oven and baking sheets, and cool on wire rack.

Makes about 5½ dozen.

Tibet

FRIED BARLEY COOKIES
SHABALÉ

(shah-bah-LAY)

In their mountainous land the Tibetans grow more barley than any other crop, and it's their staple food. Besides grinding barley into flour and using it in their cooking, they also make beer and wine from it. Barley flour has a lovely flavor and a texture that makes the cookies in this recipe quite crunchy. This is a great recipe for two people to make. While one person rolls and cuts and forms the cookies, the other person can fry them.

INGREDIENTS:

1 cup barley flour (see
    page 24)
¼ cup white flour
1 teaspoon baking soda
⅓ cup or more cold water

1 tablespoon white wine
    vegetable oil
½ cup confectioners' sugar

UTENSILS: mixing bowl, measuring cups and spoons, cooking spoons, pastry board, rolling pin, small sharp knife, ruler, heavy saucepan or wok or deep fryer, tongs, paper towels, sieve.

METHOD: Fried cookies (see page 15).

In a mixing bowl toss together barley flour, white flour, and baking powder. Add half of the cold water and all of the wine, and mix with a spoon. Add rest of water, 1 tablespoon at a time, mixing with your hands each time, until the dough just holds together.

    Sprinkle some flour on pastry board and roll out the dough ⅛ inch thick or even thinner, using a floured rolling pin. With a small sharp knife, pastry wheel, or pizza cutter cut the dough into 3-inch strips. Then cut in the opposite direction every 2 inches, so that the pieces are 3 inches by 2 inches. Cut slits across each piece with a small sharp knife so that it looks like this.

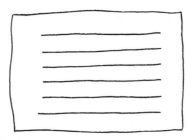

Make sure you don't cut all the way to the ends—leave a wide border.

Pick up one of the pieces and drape it over the index finger of your other hand like this.

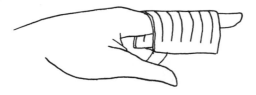

Squeeze the two ends together with your thumb pressing against the cookie and your index finger like this.

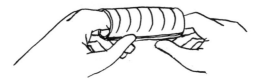

Then lift each little slashed piece with your thumb and index finger, and turn it up a little so it will stand out. Gently loosen the cookie from your finger and slide it off. Fix a few more cookies.

Ask an adult to help you with the next part of this recipe. Pour enough oil into a heavy saucepan, wok, or deep fryer so the oil is about 1½ inches deep. Place over medium heat and heat until oil is hot, but not smoking, until you can see little movements on the surface of the oil. Drop 2 or 3 cookies at a time into the hot oil, and let them fry about 1 minute, turning them over with tongs when they begin to brown lightly. When lightly browned all over, remove with tongs and put on paper towels to drain. If the oil gets too hot, turn the heat down. Continue cooking until all the cookies are fried. Turn off the flame but do not dispose of the oil until completely cooled.

Put confectioners' sugar in a sieve and sift over the drained cookies.

Makes about 2½ dozen.

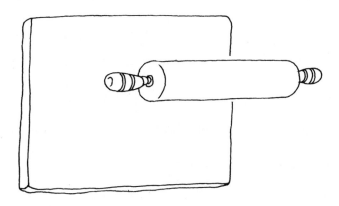

Vietnam

PRINCESS CAKES
BÁNH CÔNG CHÚA

(bahng cohng CHOO-ah)

Cookies and other sweets in Vietnam, as in most Southeast Asian and Oriental countries, are usually served alone or with tea, rather than as part of a meal. Princess Cakes are beautiful cookies made to look like little two-colored crowns such as a princess might wear. The outside colored part is hard, and the inside white part is crumbly. Princess Cakes are baked and served on little squares of white paper.

INGREDIENTS:

For the inside:
1   tablespoon mashed
      banana
½   cup melted lard
2   cups flour
½   cup sugar

For the outside:
1½ cups flour

½   cup sugar
3   tablespoons melted lard
¼   teaspoon red or green
      food coloring
¼   cup water
1   tablespoon mashed
      banana
     sesame seeds

UTENSILS: dinner plate, table fork, small saucepan, heatproof measuring cup, 2 mixing bowls, sifter, cooking spoons, measuring cups and spoons, parchment paper or white paper, scissors, ruler and pencil, baking sheets, pastry board, small sharp knife, pancake turner or spatula, wire rack.

METHOD: Shaped cookies (see page 13).

With a table fork mash a banana on a dinner plate and set aside. Put about ⅓ pound of lard in a saucepan and set over low heat. When completely melted remove from stove.

Prepare the inside of the cookies. First, measure ½ cup melted lard in a heatproof measuring cup. Pour into a mixing bowl. Sift the flour over the melted lard and mix well. Towards the end you can use your hands for mixing if you like. Add the sugar and 1 tablespoon of the mashed banana and mix well, working the ingredients together with your hands. Make 18 or 20 balls by taking pieces of the dough and molding and shaping them between your hands. The balls will be about 1¼ inches in diameter.

Using parchment paper or any other clean white paper such as typewriter paper, cut out 18 or 20 3-inch squares of paper. Arrange the squares on ungreased baking sheets with a little space between each one.

Now prepare the outside of the cakes. Sift the flour into a mixing bowl. Add the sugar and toss together. Stir the food coloring into the cold water and add to the flour-sugar mixture. Add 3 tablespoons of melted lard and 1 tablespoon of mashed banana and mix well. Use your hands to do the mixing, and then knead the dough for 1 or 2 minutes.

Sprinkle a little flour on the pastry board and turn the dough out on it. Roll the dough back and forth with the palms of your hands to form a long rope. Fold up the rope, and then roll it out again with the palms of your hands. Do this 4 times. Fold and roll out the rope again until it is 18 to 20 inches long, and is smooth and even from one end to the other. With a small sharp knife cut the dough into 1-inch slices so you will have a slice for each of the balls you've made. Use a ruler to help you measure properly.

Preheat oven at 350°. Take one slice of colored dough and flatten it between your hands, and press it out with your thumbs and fingers to make a large thin circle. Put one of the dough balls on it, and wrap the colored dough around it.

Pull and mold the edges together until the white dough does not show at all and the colored dough outside is smooth.

Place the ball on one of the squares of white paper. With the small sharp knife cut across the top of the crowns 3 times, like this, so that the top has 6 wedge-shaped cuts. Don't cut too far down or the crown will split open when it bakes. Continue making the rest of the crowns until the dough is used up. Sprinkle a few sesame seeds on top of each crown.

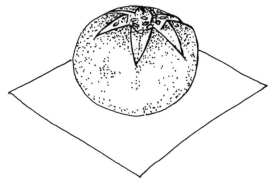

Bake 25 minutes or until the tops of the crowns are just slightly browned. Remove from oven, and place them and the white papers on wire rack to cool.
Makes 18 to 20.

Hawaii

MACADAMIA NUT–COCONUT BARS

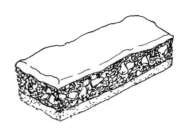

Almost all of the world's macadamia nuts are grown on the slopes of Mauna Loa, a volcano on the island of Hawaii. Macadamia nut trees were brought to Hawaii from Australia a hundred years ago. The large, round, cream-colored nuts are especially good in these cookie bars, where their flavor blends with two other Hawaiian products, pineapple juice and coconut.

INGREDIENTS:

For the bottom:
½ cup (1 stick) butter or margarine
½ cup brown sugar, firmly packed
1 egg
1¼ cups flour
¼ teaspoon salt

For the middle:
¾ cup chopped macadamia nuts (about one 3½-ounce jar)
2 eggs

1 cup brown sugar, firmly packed
1 teaspoon vanilla extract
2 tablespoons flour
¼ teaspoon salt
½ teaspoon baking powder
1½ cups flaked coconut

For the top:
1½ cups confectioners' sugar
2 tablespoons pineapple juice
1 teaspoon lemon juice

UTENSILS: 9-inch by 12-inch baking pan, 2 mixing bowls, measuring cups and spoons, cooking spoons, waxed paper, sifter, wire rack, pastry board, sharp knife with 6- to 8-inch blade or nut chopper, egg beater or wire whisk, rubber spatula, cake tester, small bowl, juice squeezer, small sharp knife, pancake turner.

METHOD: Bar cookies (see page 14).

Preheat oven at 350°. Grease and flour baking pan. In a mixing bowl cream the butter or margarine until soft. Add the brown sugar and mix well. Onto a piece of waxed paper sift together the flour and salt. Gradually add to the butter mixture, and mix until well blended. Spoon the dough into the baking pan and with floured hands pat and press the dough until it forms an even layer over the bottom of the pan.

Bake 12 minutes. Remove from oven and set the baking pan on a wire rack. Do not turn off the oven.

Chop the macadamia nuts. Break 2 eggs into a mixing bowl and beat with an egg beater or wire whisk. Gradually add the brown sugar, beating it in with the egg beater or whisk. Add the vanilla extract and stir in with a spoon. Onto a piece of waxed paper sift together the flour, salt, and baking powder. Add to the egg mixture. Add the chopped macadamia nuts and the coconut, and mix well. Spoon the mixture over the top of the baked dough in the baking pan. Smooth it out evenly with a rubber spatula.

Bake 25 minutes, or until cake tester inserted in the center of pan comes out clean. Remove from oven and set the baking pan on a wire rack. Allow to cool completely.

Sift confectioners' sugar into a small bowl. Squeeze the lemon juice and add it to the sugar, along with the pineapple juice. Mix well. Pour over the baked dough and spread evenly with a rubber spatula. Allow to stand until frosting hardens. Loosen baked cookies around edges with a pancake turner. With a small sharp knife cut into 4 pieces. Lift out the pieces with a pancake turner and set them on the pastry board. Cut each quarter into 8 pieces.
Makes 32.

Indonesia

SWEET BANANA CRISPS
REMPAH PISANG MANIS

(REHM-pah PEE-sahng MAH-nees)

A great number of unusual cookies can be found in Indonesian cooking. They range from giant, thick coconut pancakes to little boiled dough balls filled with lumps of brown palm sugar. There are fritters of all kinds—some sweet and some not at all sweet. The banana fritters in this recipe can be made with or without sugar, since the bananas have some natural sweetness themselves.

INGREDIENTS:

1 egg	*½ teaspoon cinnamon*
⅔ cup milk	*1 tablespoon brown sugar*
1 cup rice powder *	*1 banana*
1 teaspoon baking powder	*corn oil or other vegetable*
¼ teaspoon salt	*oil*

UTENSILS: mixing bowl, egg beater or whisk, measuring cups and spoons, cooking spoon, small sharp knife, frying pan, tongs, paper towels.

METHOD: Fried cookies (see page 15).

In a mixing bowl beat the egg lightly. Add the milk and stir. Stir in the rice powder, baking powder, salt, and cinnamon and stir until no lumps remain. Add the brown sugar. Slice the banana thinly and stir into the batter.

Ask an adult to help you with the next part of this recipe. Into a frying pan pour corn oil to a depth of half an inch.

* Rice powder can be bought at Oriental food stores.

Heat over a medium flame, but do not allow to become too hot or to smoke. Drop full tablespoons of batter into the oil, making 4 crisps at a time. Be sure to include 1 or 2 banana slices in each crisp. Fry about 1 minute, and turn over with tongs to brown other side. When both sides are brown remove crisps with tongs and place on paper towels to drain. Continue making crisps until all batter is used. If possible eat while hot.

Makes about 20.

Japan
SWEET AZUKI SQUARES
YOKAN
(YAH-kang)

Most little cakes, or *kashi*, made in Japanese homes are mixtures of bean paste or potato paste and sugar and are thickened with agar-agar. Agar-agar is made from seaweed and is a cross between gelatin and cornstarch in the way it makes food become firm. In Japan finished squares of *Yokan*—which look very much like our chocolate fudge—are wrapped in cherry leaves and served as a sweet with a cup of tea.

INGREDIENTS:

First step:
1 cup red azuki beans *
  cold water
1 cup sugar
1 teaspoon salt

2 cups cold water
1½ cups sugar
½ teaspoon salt

Second step:
1 stick agar-agar (about 1 inch
    by 1 inch by 11 inches) *

UTENSILS: 2 bowls, measuring cups and spoons, cooking spoons, deep saucepan, 2 medium-sized saucepans, colander, food mill or coarse strainer and wooden spoon, fine strainer, 9-inch by 9-inch baking pan, table knife.

METHOD: Bar cookies (see page 14).

First step: Put the red azuki beans in a bowl and cover them with cold water. *Let them soak overnight.*

* You can buy red azuki beans and agar-agar at health food or Oriental food stores.

Next day drain the water off the beans and put them in a deep heavy saucepan. Fill the pan three-fourths full of cold water. Put on high heat and bring to a boil. Lower the heat and simmer about 1½ hours until the bean shells break open and the beans become soft. If too much water boils away or is absorbed by the beans, add more boiling water from a teakettle. Set the colander in the sink and pour the beans into the colander to drain.

Put the beans through a food mill or push them with a wooden spoon through a coarse strainer into a bowl. Put the strained beans back in the saucepan and stir in the salt. Add the sugar gradually and mix well. Put the saucepan over medium heat and cook, stirring constantly, until the paste becomes very thick and leaves the sides of the pan when you stir. Remove pan from stove.

Second step: Put cold water in another saucepan. Break the agar-agar stick into the water, and bring to a boil over medium heat, stirring constantly. When the agar-agar has melted add the sugar and stir until dissolved. Pour through a fine strainer into a clean saucepan. Add the salt and the bean paste and stir until smooth. Put over medium heat and cook, stirring every minute or two, for about 20 minutes, until the mixture becomes thickened and looks something like chocolate pudding. Pour cooked mixture into baking pan and allow to sit until completely cool. Cut into pieces about 1½ inches square.

Makes about 3 dozen.

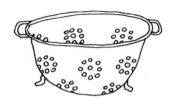

Philippines

PEANUT SQUARES
PASTILLAS DE MANÍ

(pah-STEE-yahs deh mah-NEE)

In the Philippines *Pastillas de Maní* are made with native-grown peanuts. They are really more like candies than cookies. They should be made from whole roasted peanuts for they won't turn out properly if you make them with peanut butter. *Pastillas de Maní*, and many other sweets, are eaten in the Philippines at *merienda,* a late afternoon snack time that has been a tradition in the islands since the days of Spanish rule there. *Merienda* is a popular way of entertaining among Filipinos, who usually serve hot chocolate or an iced coconut drink called *halo-halo* with the sweets.

INGREDIENTS:

1 cup shelled roasted
    peanuts
½ cup sugar

¾ cup milk
¼ cup sugar for pastry board

UTENSILS: meat grinder, measuring cups, saucepan, cooking spoon, pastry board, metal spatula, rolling pin, small sharp knife.

METHOD: Roll and cut cookies (see page 14).

Put the peanuts through a meat grinder with a medium blade. Put them in a saucepan with the ½ cup sugar and the milk, and mix well.

Place over medium flame and cook, stirring constantly, until the mixture boils and the sugar dissolves. Lower the flame and cook, stirring often, until the mixture thickens. As the mixture becomes very thick stir continually, to prevent sticking. This takes about 15 minutes. When the mixture is so thick that you can see the bottom of the pan when you stir, remove from stove.

Sprinkle the ¼ cup sugar on a pastry board. Turn the peanut mixture out onto the sugar, and flatten it out with a metal spatula. Allow to stand until it is cool enough to touch. Roll it out with a rolling pin to about ¼ inch thick. With a small sharp knife cut into small squares, or if you prefer, cut out with small cookie cutters. Remove with a spatula and arrange on a plate.

Makes about 3½ to 4 dozen.

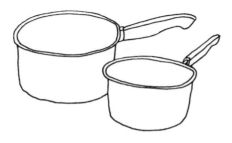

Australia

GOLDEN SYRUP COOKIES
ANZACS

Anzac is a nickname for someone who comes from Australia or New Zealand. The word comes from the initial letters of the Australian and New Zealand Army Corps. During World War I, Australian and New Zealand soldiers were nicknamed ANZACS, and somewhere along the line these very popular cookies were also given the name. Australia is part of the British Commonwealth so it isn't surprising that some of the Anzac ingredients are typically British; golden syrup comes from England, and oatmeal is a favorite throughout the British Isles.

INGREDIENTS:

½ cup (1 stick) butter or margarine
2 tablespoons golden syrup (such as Lyle's)
1 cup flour
½ teaspoon baking powder

½ cup sugar
1½ cups flaked coconut
1½ cups rolled oats (uncooked)
1 tablespoon milk

UTENSILS: baking sheets, mixing bowl, measuring cups and spoons, cooking spoons, waxed paper, sifter, spatula or pancake turner, wire rack.

METHOD: Shaped cookies (see page 13)

Preheat oven at 350°. Grease baking sheets. In a mixing bowl cream the butter or margarine until soft. Add the golden syrup and mix well.

Onto a piece of waxed paper sift together the flour, baking

powder, and sugar. Add to the butter mixture and combine well. Add the coconut and rolled oats and mix well. Add the milk and mix.

Roll small pieces of the dough between the palms of your hands to make balls about 1¼ inches in diameter. Arrange on baking sheets. Bake 15 minutes. Remove from oven and baking sheets, and cool on wire rack.

Makes about 3 dozen.

Cookies from
North America
and the West Indies

Canada

MAPLE-SUGARING-TIME COOKIES

In Canada's Province of Quebec there's a big maple sugar industry, just as there is in our country in New York State and Vermont. In early springtime when the snow is still on the ground, the sap begins to rise in the sugar maple trees. The trees are tapped by drilling little holes in the trunks and letting the sap drip out into buckets. Then the sap is collected and boiled down to make maple syrup or maple sugar, from which these cookies are made.

INGREDIENTS:
- *½ cup chopped walnuts or other nuts (see page 21)*
- *½ cup bacon drippings or ½ pound bacon*
- *1 egg*
- *1 cup pure maple syrup*
- *1½ cups flour*
- *1 teaspoon salt*
- *2 teaspoons baking powder*
- *1 teaspoon nutmeg*
- *½ cup raisins*
- *1½ cups rolled oats (uncooked)*
- *¼ cup milk*

UTENSILS: baking sheets, sharp knife with 6- to 8-inch blade or nut chopper, small saucepan, heatproof measuring cup, mixing bowl, egg beater or wire whisk, cooking spoons, waxed paper, sifter, measuring cups and spoons, spatula or pancake turner, wire rack.

METHOD: Drop cookies (see page 13).

Sauté ½ pound bacon or melt bacon drippings in a small saucepan over low heat. Remove from heat and measure out ½ cup in a heatproof measuring cup. Allow to cool for 10 minutes.

Preheat oven at 375°. Grease baking sheets. Chop nuts.

Break the egg into a mixing bowl and beat lightly with an egg beater or wire whisk. Add the maple syrup and stir well. Add the bacon fat and stir well.

Onto a piece of waxed paper sift together the flour, salt, baking powder, and nutmeg. Gradually add to the maple mixture, mixing well. Stir in the raisins and rolled oats. Add the milk and chopped nuts and mix well.

Drop dough by teaspoonfuls on baking sheets and bake 10 minutes until edges are lightly browned. Remove from oven and baking sheets, and cool on wire rack.

Makes about 5 dozen.

Northwest United States and Alaska
SOURDOUGH COOKIES

When pioneers crossed our country to settle the West one of the most valuable things they included in their provisions was a sourdough pot. Commercial yeast and baking powder weren't available in those days, and the settlers used sourdough to make raised bread and biscuits. Sourdough, a mixture of airborne wild yeast, flour, and water, was such an essential part of the lives of Alaska's explorers, traders, prospectors, and gold miners that the men themselves became known as "sourdoughs." The sturdy hotcakes and biscuits the "sourdoughs" ate helped them to do their hard work and live through Alaska's bitter cold winters. During the 1800s western chuck wagon cooks used sourdough in baking for the cowhands during the months-long cattle drives to the rail terminals. Most of the best sourdough bread today comes from San Francisco, where it's been a specialty for many decades. Once you make your sourdough starter save a cup of it each time you bake, and you can keep your sourdough going forever.

INGREDIENTS:

For the sourdough starter:
1 package active dry yeast
2 cups warm water
2 cups flour

For the cookies:
1 cup sourdough starter

4 eggs
¾ cup (1½ sticks) butter or
  margarine
1 cup sugar
1 teaspoon vanilla extract
3 cups flour
1 teaspoon salt

UTENSILS: *For the starter—large bowl, measuring cups, cooking spoon, clean dish towel, 1-pint glass jar with tight-fitting screw-on lid. For the cookies—small saucepan, measuring cups and spoons, cooking spoons, egg beater or wire whisk, waxed paper, sifter, baking sheets, spatula or pancake turner, wire rack, mixing bowl.*

METHOD: Drop cookies (see page 13).

First make the sourdough starter. Measure 2 cups of warm water from the hot water faucet and put it in a large bowl. The water should be warm enough to feel comfortable when you sprinkle some on the inside of your wrist, but not hot enough to hurt you. Sprinkle the package of yeast over the water and stir until it dissolves. Add the 2 cups flour and mix until quite smooth. Cover the bowl loosely with a clean dish towel and set it in a warm place, without disturbing, *for two days,* or until the mixture gets bubbly and separates.

Preheat oven at 350°. Grease baking sheets.
The cookies: In a small saucepan melt the butter or margarine over low heat. Remove from heat.

Break the eggs into a mixing bowl and beat lightly with an egg beater or wire whisk. Stir the sourdough starter until it is perfectly smooth and well blended. Measure 1 cup of the starter and add to the eggs, mixing well.

Put the rest of the starter in a glass jar, screw the lid on tightly, and store the jar in the refrigerator.

Add the melted butter or margarine to the egg-sourdough mixture and mix well. Add the sugar and vanilla extract and mix well.

Onto a piece of waxed paper sift the flour and salt together. Add to the dough gradually, mixing well each time.

Drop by heaping teaspoonfuls onto the baking sheets, and

bake 12 to 15 minutes until cookies have a brown edge. Remove from oven and baking sheets, and cool on wire rack. **Makes about 5½ dozen.**

To make sourdough cookies again:

You will need to start the day before baking to replenish the starter. Remove the jar of sourdough starter from the refrigerator. Empty it into a large bowl. Add 1 cup warm water and mix well. Add 1 cup flour and mix well. (You don't need to add any more yeast.) Cover the bowl loosely with a clean dish towel, and let it stand overnight in a warm place. The next day make the cookies same as before. You will always have sourdough starter for making cookies if you use this method. You should use the starter every two weeks to keep the yeast active. (The sourdough starter is also good for making sourdough bread, pancakes, and biscuits.)

Midwest United States

AMERICAN INDIAN WILD RICE CAKES

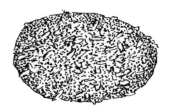

Wild rice was one of the favorite foods of the Dakota, Menomini, and Ojibwa tribes who lived in the territory that is now Minnesota. It is not really rice, but the seeds of a tall grass that grows along the edges of rivers and streams. The Indians went out in pairs in their canoes, one paddling, the other bending the stalks of grass over the canoe and beating off the seeds with a stick so they fell into the canoe bottom. The Indians boiled the wild rice, and used it to stuff birds or to make into cakes. According to a record left by a fur trader in the early days of the West, some Indians mixed the wild rice with bear fat and sugar to make a sweet. Some wild rice is cultivated today, but most of it still grows wild in Minnesota and still has to be gathered by hand, which makes it very expensive.

INGREDIENTS:
1 cup wild rice
4 cups water
1 teaspoon salt
¼ cup cornmeal (stone-
ground if possible)

1 or 2 tablespoons bacon
drippings or vegetable
oil

UTENSILS: measuring cups and spoons, sieve, saucepan, cooking spoon, frying pan, pancake turner, paper towels.

METHOD: Shaped cookies (see page 13).

Put the wild rice in a sieve and wash it under cold running

water. Put it in a saucepan with the water and salt. Bring to boil over high heat. Reduce heat and simmer, uncovered, about 35 minutes until rice is tender but not mushy. Gradually add the cornmeal and mix well. Remove from heat and cool until mixture is comfortable to the touch. Shape into 12 flat cakes, 2½ to 3 inches in diameter.

Melt bacon drippings in frying pan or pour in an equal amount of vegetable oil. Sauté half of the cakes until brown on one side, turn with pancake turner, and brown on the other side. Drain on paper towels. Sauté the rest of the cakes and drain on paper towels. Serve the wild rice cakes hot or cold.

Makes 12.

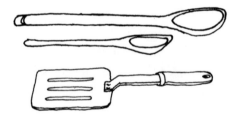

Northeast United States

JOE FROGGERS

Uncle Joe was a black man who lived a long time ago in Marblehead on the coast of Massachusetts. He made his living baking great quantities of huge cookies and selling them to the fishing fleets sailing out from Marblehead. His cookies were known to stay fresh for many months while the fishermen were at sea, and they became great local favorites. Uncle Joe's cookies were so big and fat that people said they looked a lot like the plump frogs that lived in the pond in front of his house, and that's how they came to be known as Joe Froggers. You may have tasted some of these cookies if you've traveled to parts of Massachusetts where they've begun to bake them again.

INGREDIENTS:
¼ cup molasses
¾ teaspoon baking soda
½ cup water
¼ teaspoon rum extract
3¾ cups flour
1 teaspoon ground ginger
½ teaspoon ground cloves
1 teaspoon salt
½ cup (1 stick) butter or
*   margarine*
1 cup sugar

UTENSILS: small bowl, measuring cups and spoons, cooking spoons, waxed paper, sifter, mixing bowl, plastic wrap or aluminum foil, piece of cardboard and pencil, scissors, ruler, 3 baking sheets, pastry board, rolling pin, small sharp knife, spatula or pancake turner, wire rack.

METHOD: Roll and cut cookies (see page 14).

Combine the molasses and baking soda in a small bowl. Add

the rum extract to the water. Onto a piece of waxed paper sift together the flour, ginger, cloves, and salt.

In a mixing bowl cream the butter or margarine until soft. Gradually add the sugar and mix well. Stir in about one third of the flour mixture. Now add the molasses mixture and mix well. Add another third of the flour mixture and mix well. Stir in the water-rum mixture. Add the remaining flour mixture and stir until well combined. Cover the bowl with plastic wrap or aluminum foil and place in refrigerator overnight.

On a piece of cardboard draw a circle about 5 inches in diameter, using a small plate or any round object of the correct size to trace around. Cut out the circle to use as a pattern for cutting out cookies the next day.

Next day preheat oven at 375°. Grease baking sheets. Sprinkle a little flour on the pastry board. Put the dough on the board, flour the rolling pin, and roll out the dough about ½ inch thick. Cut out the cookies by laying the cardboard pattern on the dough and cutting around it with a small sharp pointed knife. Put all the scraps together for the last cookie. Place 2 cookies on each baking sheet and bake 15 minutes. Don't bake them longer or they'll get hard. Remove from oven and baking sheets, and cool on wire rack.
Makes 6.

Southern United States
TAVERN BISCUITS

This recipe for tavern biscuits comes from a cookbook written by a lady in Virginia more than a century ago. She wrote it like this:

To one pound of flour, add half a pound of sugar, half a pound of butter, some mace and nutmeg powdered, and a glass of brandy or wine; wet it with milk, and when well kneaded, roll it thin, cut it in shapes, and bake it quickly.

It's quite different from the way we write recipes today. For instance, no oven temperature was mentioned because it was almost impossible to make wood- or coal-burning stoves stay at a certain temperature and burn evenly. Quantities of ingredients were usually given in weights, like pounds and ounces, rather than in measurements like cups and tablespoons. Sometimes no quantity was mentioned, and the recipe would just say to add "some."

INGREDIENTS:
½ cup (1 stick) butter or   *¼ teaspoon nutmeg*
    margarine   *⅛ teaspoon mace*
1 cup sugar   *¼ cup red wine*
2 cups flour

UTENSILS: baking sheets, measuring spoons and cups, mixing bowl, cooking spoon, waxed paper, sifter, pastry board, rolling pin, cookie cutters, spatula or pancake turner, wire rack.

METHOD: Roll and cut cookies (see page 14).

Preheat oven at 350°. Grease baking sheets. Cream the butter or margarine in a mixing bowl until soft. Gradually add sugar and combine well.

Onto a piece of waxed paper sift together the flour, nutmeg, and mace. Add half the flour mixture to the butter and mix well. Add the wine and mix well. Add the rest of the flour mixture and stir until well combined. Put in refrigerator 1 hour to chill.

Sprinkle a little flour on the pastry board. Turn out the dough on the board and knead with your hands until smooth. Roll out with floured rolling pin until ¼ inch thick or less. Cut out cookies with cookie cutters and arrange on baking sheets.

Bake 10 to 12 minutes until lightly browned. Remove from oven and baking sheets, and cool on wire rack.

Makes 3½ to 4 dozen.

Mexico

CHEESE COOKIES
TAPABOCAS

(tah-pah-BOH-cahs)

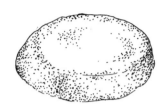

No European had ever tasted vanilla or chocolate until Spanish explorers came to ancient Mexico and discovered the Aztec royalty drinking frothy cups of snow-chilled chocolate flavored with vanilla and sweetened with honey. In the sixteenth century when Spanish nuns came to Mexico with the settlers, they brought cinnamon, cloves, sugar, and flour with them and created many cakes and desserts for which colonial Mexico became famous. The cookies in our recipe are flavored with cheese and sherry, a Spanish wine, and are very good with a cup of hot chocolate made in the Mexican manner. Make some hot chocolate and flavor it with cinnamon, sugar, and even ground almonds if you like. Before you serve the hot chocolate beat it hard with an egg beater to make it very foamy. *Tapabocas*, by the way, means "mouth silencers" in Spanish.

INGREDIENTS:

2 cups flour
¼ cup sugar
½ cup (1 stick) butter or
*   margarine*
½ cup coarsely grated
*   Muenster or Monterey*
*   Jack cheese*

1 egg
3 tablespoons sherry wine

UTENSILS: baking sheets, mixing bowl, sifter, measuring cups and spoons, table knife, grater, small bowl, egg beater or wire whisk, cooking spoon, spatula or pancake turner, wire rack.

METHOD: Shaped cookies (see page 13).

Preheat oven at 350°. Grease baking sheets. Into a mixing bowl sift together the flour and sugar. Cut the butter or margarine into small pieces and add it to the flour mixture. Grate the cheese and pack it loosely into measuring cup to ½ cup mark. Add to the flour mixture. Toss the ingredients in the bowl with your fingers and rub them together until they are all crumbly and well blended.

In a small bowl break the egg, and beat it lightly with egg beater or wire whisk. Mix in the sherry wine. Add to the flour mixture and mix well with a spoon or with your hands.

Take small pieces of dough, about a teaspoon at a time, and shape into balls between the palms of your hands. Arrange on baking sheets. Press cookies gently with the palm of your hand to flatten a little. Bake 12 to 13 minutes until lightly browned. Remove from oven and baking sheets, and cool on wire rack.

Makes about 4 dozen.

Cuba

MATANZAS SUGAR COOKIES
POLVORONES MATANCEROS

(pohl-voh-ROH-nehs mah-tahn-SEH-rohs)

The recipe for these cookies comes from the Province of Matanzas, just east of Havana. From this point all across the gently rolling countryside to the far eastern end of Cuba grows the sugarcane for which Cuba has been so well known for centuries. Cuban sugarcane produces a higher yield of sugar per plant than is produced anywhere else in the world. Sugar, coffee, and tobacco are the three leading crops in Cuba, and sugar accounts for 90 percent of its exports. Cuban coffee is rich and dark, and the Cubans like to drink it sweetened with lots of Cuban sugar and accompanied by a plate of *Matanzas* sugar cookies.

INGREDIENTS:

1   *cup vegetable shortening,*   1½ *teaspoons vanilla extract*
      such as Spry or Crisco   4   *cups flour*
1   *cup sugar*   ½   *teaspoon salt*
2   *eggs*   ½   *teaspoon baking powder*

UTENSILS: baking sheets, bowl, measuring cups and spoons, cooking spoons, waxed paper, sifter, pastry board, rolling pin, round cookie cutter 2 inches in diameter, spatula or pancake turner, wire rack.

METHOD: Roll and cut cookies (see page 14).

Preheat oven at 350°. Grease baking sheets. In a mixing bowl cream the vegetable shortening until soft. Add the sugar gradually and mix well. Add the eggs and vanilla extract and mix well.

Onto a piece of waxed paper sift the flour, salt, and baking powder. Gradually add to the shortening-egg mixture, mixing well each time. Divide the dough in half.

Put a piece of waxed paper about 18 inches long on the pastry board. Put half of the dough on the waxed paper. Put another 18-inch-long piece of waxed paper on top of the dough. Press down with your hands gently to flatten the dough slightly. With a rolling pin roll the dough out between the two pieces of waxed paper until it is a little less than ¼ inch thick. Peel off the top piece of waxed paper.

Cut out cookies with cookie cutter. Peel them off the waxed paper and arrange on baking sheets. Bake 10 to 12 minutes until lightly browned. Remove from oven and baking sheets, and cool on wire rack. Roll out, cut, and bake other half of dough in the same way.

Makes about 6 dozen.

Curaçao
SPONGE COOKIES
PANLEVI

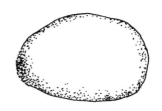

(pahn-LEH-vee)

When the Sephardic Jews fled from Spain and Portugal to escape religious persecution hundreds of years ago, some of them settled on the Caribbean island of Curaçao in the Netherland Antilles. They brought with them not only their religion but also a heritage of recipes, cooking habits, and dietary customs. Their recipes have been handed down through the generations, and one that survives today is *Panlevi*. This is a cookie traditionally served with hot chocolate at certain Jewish religious celebrations on the island. It's also a favorite of children of all religions who live in Curaçao.

INGREDIENTS:

4 *eggs*	1 *teaspoon vanilla extract*
1 *cup sugar*	2½ *cups flour*
¼ *teaspoon mace*	*pinch of salt*

UTENSILS: baking sheets, mixing bowl, egg beater or wire whisk, measuring cups and spoons, cooking spoons, sifter, waxed paper, rubber spatula, spatula or pancake turner, wire rack.

METHOD: Drop cookies (see page 13).

Preheat oven at 325°. Grease and flour baking sheets. Break eggs into mixing bowl and beat with egg beater until frothy. Gradually add sugar, mixing with a spoon. Stir in mace and vanilla.

Onto a piece of waxed paper sift together the flour and salt. Add to egg mixture and fold in gently but thoroughly with a rubber spatula. Drop by tablespoonfuls on baking sheets. Bake 20 minutes or until edges are lightly browned. Remove from oven, baking sheets, and cool on wire rack. **Makes about 20.**

Jamaica

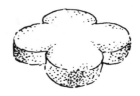

ARROWROOT BISCUITS

Many unusual foods grow on the tropical islands of the West Indies. The star apple, a fruit which grows in Jamaica, is known here in American markets as ugli fruit. It is wrinkled and funny looking outside and like a sweet grapefruit inside. There are also cashew nuts, which grow as part of cashew apples which are the fruit of the cashew tree. Allspice, a berry that tastes like a combination of many spices, also grows in Jamaica. Arrowroot is the root of a plant that grows throughout the islands, and is ground into a powder to use in cooking and baking. It's easier to digest than other starches, and it makes nice light cookies like the ones in this recipe.

INGREDIENTS:

2 tablespoons butter	*1 cup flour*
⅓ cup sugar	*¼ teaspoon baking powder*
2 eggs	*¼ teaspoon salt*
½ cup arrowroot	

UTENSILS: mixing bowl, measuring cups and spoons, cooking spoons, small bowl, egg beater or wire whisk, waxed paper, sifter, baking sheets, pastry board, rolling pin, small cookie cutter, spatula or pancake turner, wire rack.

METHOD: Roll and cut cookies (see page 14).

Cream the butter in a mixing bowl until soft. Add the sugar and mix well. Break the eggs into a small bowl and beat lightly with an egg beater or wire whisk. Add them to the dough and mix until well blended.

Onto a piece of waxed paper sift together the arrowroot,

flour, baking powder, and salt. Gradually add to the butter and egg mixture, and mix well. Place in refrigerator for 30 minutes to chill.

Preheat oven at 350°. Grease baking sheets. Sprinkle a little flour on a pastry board and roll out the dough with a floured rolling pin until it is less than ⅛ inch thick. Cut out cookies with a small cookie cutter and arrange on baking sheets.

Bake 6 to 7 minutes until faintly brown. Remove from oven and baking sheets, and cool on wire rack.

Makes about 7½ dozen.

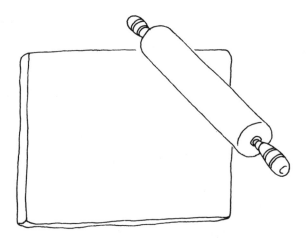

Puerto Rico

RUM LARD COOKIES
MANTECADOS CON RON

(mahn-teh-CAH-dohs cohn ROHN)

Sugar is one of Puerto Rico's most important agricultural crops, and the making of rum is one of its main industries. Rum is made from molasses, a by-product of sugar, and it has been produced on a number of Caribbean islands, including Puerto Rico, Jamaica, and Cuba, since the sixteenth century. When Columbus made his second voyage to the New World in 1493 he brought sugarcane roots with him from Europe. They were planted on the island of Haiti, and from there sugarcane production and rum manufacturing spread throughout the Caribbean.

INGREDIENTS:

2 cups flour	*½ cup lard*
pinch of salt	*¼ cup Puerto Rican or other*
1 cup sugar	*rum*

UTENSILS: baking sheets, measuring cups, sifter, mixing bowl, cooking spoon, table knife, spatula or pancake turner, wire rack.

METHOD: Shaped cookies (see page 13).

Preheat oven at 400°. Grease baking sheets. Into a mixing bowl sift together the flour and salt. Add the sugar and toss together. Cut the lard into small pieces and add it to the flour mixture. Work and rub the ingredients together with your fingers until well blended. Add the rum and mix quickly with a spoon until smooth and well blended.

Take pieces of dough about the size of a large marble and press and roll them between the palms of your hands to make balls. Arrange on baking sheets and press down with your hands to flatten.

Bake 10 minutes until very lightly browned. Remove from oven and baking sheets, and cool on wire rack.

Makes about 2½ dozen.

Cookies from
Central America
and South America

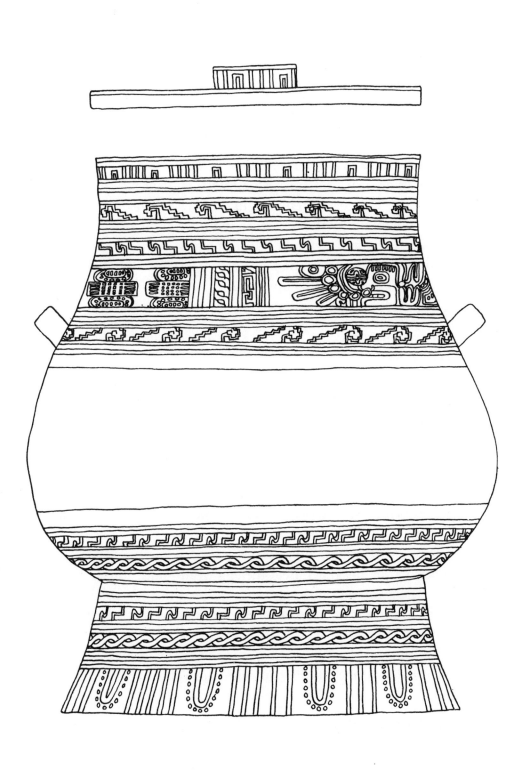

Costa Rica

BAPTISMAL COOKIES
MANON DEL BAUTISMO
(mah-NOHN dehl ba-oo-TEES-moh)

These little cakes are the traditional sweet served at baptismal celebrations in Costa Rica, along with cups of steaming hot chocolate. The cornstarch used in the recipe gives *Manon del Bautismo* an unusual dry texture quite different from cookies made with flour. The Costa Ricans make *Manon del Bautismo* in tiny baking tins shaped in pretty patterns, but you can bake them in very small cupcake tins.

INGREDIENTS:

2 cups cornstarch
¾ cup sugar

¼ teaspoon cinnamon
6 eggs

UTENSILS: very small cupcake tins, sifter, waxed paper, measuring cups and spoons, mixing bowl, small bowl, egg beater, rubber spatula, cooking spoon, wire rack, table knife.

METHOD: Cupcakes (see page 15).

Preheat oven at 350°. Grease cupcake tins. Onto a piece of waxed paper sift together the cornstarch, sugar, and cinnamon.

Separate the eggs. Put the whites in a mixing bowl, and the yolks in a smaller bowl. Beat the egg whites until stiff, but not dry. Then use the same egg beater to beat the egg yolks until thick. With a rubber spatula turn the whites onto the yolks, and fold in gently.

Sift the cornstarch mixture over the egg mixture, about one quarter at a time, folding in with the rubber spatula each time.

Spoon the dough into the tins until they are a little more than half full. Bake 20 minutes until lightly browned. Remove tins from oven and set on a wire rack. When cool enough to touch remove the cakes from the tins and allow them to cool completely on the wire rack. If necessary use a table knife to remove the cakes from the tins.

Makes about 3 dozen.

Panama

SIGHS
SUSPIROS
(soo-SPEE-rohs)

Suspiros means "sighs" in Spanish, and cookies by this name are found in many Spanish-speaking countries in Central and South America. Each country seems to have its own idea of what a "sigh" should be. Some *Suspiros* are pale, airy, egg-white meringues; some are made with nuts; some are swirled high or mounded up or twisted into coils. Panama's version is made with egg yolks and uses cornstarch instead of flour. The dough is rolled into ropes and coiled into pinwheels before baking.

INGREDIENTS:

½ cup (1 stick) butter or	*2 egg yolks*
margarine	*¼ teaspoon cinnamon*
1 cup sugar	*2 cups cornstarch*

UTENSILS: baking sheets, mixing bowl, measuring cups and spoons, cooking spoon, cup, sifter, waxed paper, ruler, spatula or pancake turner, wire rack.

METHOD: Shaped cookies (see page 13).

Preheat oven at 350°. Grease baking sheets. Cream butter or margarine in a mixing bowl until soft. Gradually add the sugar and mix well.

Separate 2 eggs. Put the whites in a cup and save for another use. Add the yolks and cinnamon to the butter and sugar and mix well.

Sift the cornstarch onto a piece of waxed paper, and measure. Gradually add to dough, mixing well. When dough becomes difficult to mix with a spoon, mix with your hands.

When the dough is well mixed take pieces about the size of a large marble and roll back and forth on the table with the palms of your hands to form ropes about as thick as a pencil and about 9 inches long. Use the ruler to measure the length. Starting from the center form the ropes into pinwheel shapes on the baking sheets like this.

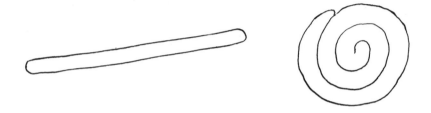

Bake 10 to 12 minutes until lightly browned. Remove from oven and baking sheets, and cool on wire rack.
Makes about 3 dozen.

Argentina

QUINCE CRESCENTS
CRECIENTES DE MEMBRILLO
(creh-cee-YEHN-tehs deh mehm-BREE-yoh)

Quinces are such a tart fruit that they are rarely eaten raw. With sugar, however, they make excellent jelly, jam, preserves, and fruit desserts. In Argentina, quinces are often cooked with sugar to make a paste that is thicker than jam. Quince paste is used for stuffing pastries and filling cookies as we do in this recipe. You can buy quince paste at Latin American food stores or specialty food shops. If you can't find quince paste use quince jam or preserves (not jelly) which you can buy in grocery stores or supermarkets.

INGREDIENTS:

1½ *cups flour*
½ *teaspoon baking powder*
½ *teaspoon salt*
½ *cup (1 stick) butter or margarine*

3 *tablespoons cold water*
1 *cup quince paste*
½ *cup confectioners' sugar*

UTENSILS: *measuring cups and spoons, baking sheets, round cookie cutter or cardboard circle 3½ inches in diameter, small sharp knife, sifter, mixing bowl, table knife, cooking spoon, pastry board, rolling pin, table fork, spatula or pancake turner, wire rack, sieve.*

METHOD: Roll and cut cookies (see page 14).

Preheat oven at 350°. Grease baking sheets. Into a mixing bowl sift together the flour, baking powder, and salt. Cut the butter or margarine into small pieces and put them in the bowl with the flour. With your fingers blend and work the ingredients together until they look even and crumbly. Measure 3 tablespoons of very cold water from the faucet, and stir into the butter-flour mixture. With your hands gather the dough together and press it into a ball. Sprinkle a little flour on a pastry board and roll out the dough with a floured rolling pin until it is ⅛ inch thick. Cut cookies with a cookie cutter or by tracing around a cardboard circle with a sharp pointed knife. Lift away the extra dough.

Put a heaping teaspoon of quince paste on each circle. Wet your finger with cold water from the faucet, then wet the edges of a circle with your finger. Fold the circle over to form a half-circle, or crescent. Press down the open edge with your fingers. With a fork press down the edges again. With a pancake turner transfer the filled crescent to the baking sheet. Repeat with the other circles, arranging about 8 on each sheet.

Bake 18 to 20 minutes, or until lightly browned. Remove from oven and baking sheets, and cool on wire rack. Put the confectioners' sugar in a sieve and sift it over the cooled crescents.

Makes about 22.

Bolivia

CARAMEL-FILLED COOKIES
ALFAJORES

(ahl-fah-HAW-rehs)

Alfajores are popular at four o'clock, tea time in Bolivia. The filling is cinnamon flavored and caramel-like in consistency, and takes an hour or longer to make. Bolivians like to make a large batch of this filling and keep some on hand for desserts, frosting, filling for cakes and cookies, or spreads for crackers, toast, or bread. *Alfajores* are rich and bright yellow in color from the many egg yolks in them. They are best when eaten the day they're baked.

INGREDIENTS:

For the filling:

6 tablespoons chopped
    walnuts or pecans
    (see page 21)
2 cups milk
½ cup sugar
    pinch of baking soda
1 2-inch cinnamon stick
½ teaspoon vanilla extract

For the cookies:

5 egg yolks
1½ teaspoons sugar
2 tablespoons butter
1½ teaspoons Pisco liquor,
    or brandy, or rum
1 cup flour
3 tablespoons
    confectioners' sugar

UTENSILS: For the filling—cutting board and sharp knife with 6- to 8-inch blade or nut chopper, measuring cups and spoons, saucepan, wooden cooking spoon. For the cookies—bowl, mixing bowl, egg beater or wire whisk, measuring cups and spoons, small saucepan, cooking spoon, waxed paper, sifter, pastry board, rolling pin, round cookie cutter with fancy edge if possible, table fork, baking sheets, spatula or pancake turner, wire rack, sieve.

METHOD: Roll and cut cookies (see page 14).

The filling: Chop the nuts very finely. Combine in a saucepan the milk, sugar, baking soda, and cinnamon stick. Place over medium heat and cook, stirring constantly, until mixture begins to boil. Turn heat down to low immediately, and simmer gently for 1 hour and 30 minutes, or until the mixture becomes as thick as very heavy cream and brownish in color. Stir it about every 10 minutes while it cooks. When thick, remove from heat and allow to cool for 10 minutes. Remove cinnamon stick. Stir in vanilla. Let filling sit until completely cool. It will get thicker as it cools. Stir in nuts. If you aren't making the cookies right away, spoon the filling into a glass jar, cover tightly with a lid, and store in the refrigerator.

To make the cookies, separate 5 eggs. Put the whites in a bowl and save for another use. Put yolks in a mixing bowl and beat well with an egg beater. Add sugar and beat again.

Preheat oven at 350°. In a small saucepan melt the butter over a very low flame. Remove from heat and add, a little at a time, to the egg yolk mixture, beating each time with the egg beater. Add the Pisco liquor or brandy or rum, and stir with a spoon.

Onto a piece of waxed paper sift the flour. Measure and sift again gradually, into the egg mixture, mixing well each time.

Sprinkle a little flour on a pastry board and with a floured rolling pin roll out the dough as thin as you can roll it. Cut out cookies with the round cookie cutter. Lift away extra dough. If your cookie cutter does not have a fancy edge, then go around the edge of each cookie with a fork to make fancy marks. Arrange the cookies on ungreased baking sheets and bake 7 to 9 minutes. Do not let the cookies get brown. Remove from oven and baking sheets, and cool on wire rack.

With a table knife spread some of the cooled filling on half of the cookies. Put the remaining cookies on top to make sandwiches. Sift confectioners' sugar over the cookie sandwiches.

Makes about 1½ dozen.

Brazil

BRAZIL NUT SANDWICHES
DOCINHOS DO PARÁ

(daw-SEE-nawsh daw pah-RAH)

Only in the tropical rain forests of Brazil's Amazon basin do Brazil nut trees grow wild. These straight, towering trees have great leathery leaves a foot or two long. One tree can produce as many as a thousand pounds of Brazil nuts in a year. While people have tried to cultivate Brazil nut trees they've found it doesn't pay, since it takes about twelve years for the trees to begin growing nuts. Almost all Brazil nuts are shipped out of Brazil through the port of Pará, and the name of the nut in Portuguese, the language of Brazil, is *castanha do Pará,* or "chestnut of Pará." The Brazilians make all sorts of lovely sweets using Brazil nuts, and this cookie is one typically served there for afternoon tea or coffee.

INGREDIENTS:

½ *cup (1 stick) butter or*
    margarine
⅓ *cup sugar*
½ *cup cornstarch*

½ *cup flour*
½ *cup ground Brazil nuts*
    (see page 21)
jelly or jam

UTENSILS: measuring cups, mixing bowl, cooking spoons, sifter, waxed paper, baking sheets, pastry board, rolling pin, round cookie cutter 2 inches in diameter with fancy edges if possible, spatula or pancake turner, wire rack, table knife.

METHOD: Roll and cut cookies (see page 14).

Cream butter or margarine in a mixing bowl until soft. Add the sugar and mix well.

    Sift together onto a piece of waxed paper the cornstarch

and flour. Gradually add to the butter and sugar mixture, mixing well. Add the ground Brazil nuts and mix well. Chill in the refrigerator for 1 hour, or in the freezer for 15 minutes.

Preheat oven at 325°. Grease baking sheets. Sprinkle a little flour on a pastry board and use a floured rolling pin to roll out the dough until it is about ⅛ inch thick. With a cookie cutter cut out circles. Transfer to baking sheets with a spatula or pancake turner.

Bake 12 minutes until just lightly browned. Remove from oven and very carefully take cookies from baking sheets with spatula or pancake turner. Cool on wire rack.

When cool, turn over half the cookies and spread them with any kind of jelly or jam that you like. Put the remaining cookies on top, sandwich fashion.
Makes about 2 dozen.

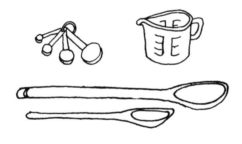

Colombia

DARK SUGAR COOKIES
CUCAS

(KOO-kahs)

This is a very old recipe that comes from the area of Antioquia and Caldas in the central-western part of Colombia. In Colombia *Cucas* are made with *panela* as a sweetener, instead of the dark brown sugar we're using in our recipe. *Panela*, which has a delicious rich flavor, is made from cane sugar and formed into extremely hard blocks that have to be chopped up with a knife and mallet to use for cooking. For *Cucas* the *panela* is cooked in water until it melts before being added to the recipe. For special occasions *Cucas* are spread with a peanut frosting.

INGREDIENTS:

For the cookies:
2   cups flour
½   teaspoon baking powder
½   cup (1 stick) butter
1   pound dark brown sugar
2   eggs

For the frosting:
1½ cups peanuts
¾   cup (1½ sticks) butter
3   cups confectioners' sugar
1   tablespoon milk

UTENSILS: For the cookies—baking sheets, sifter, waxed paper, measuring cups and spoons, cooking spoon, mixing bowl, pastry board, rolling pin, pizza cutter or pastry wheel or small sharp knife, ruler, dinner fork, pancake turner or spatula, wire rack. For the frosting—cutting board and sharp knife with 6- to 8-inch blade or nut chopper, measuring cups and spoons, mixing bowl, cooking spoon, sifter, table knife.

METHOD: Roll and cut cookies (see page 14).

Preheat oven at 325°. Grease baking sheets. Sift together onto a piece of waxed paper the flour and baking powder.

Cream the butter in a mixing bowl until soft. Gradually add the dark brown sugar, stirring well each time. Add 1 egg and mix well. Add about a third of the flour mixture, and stir some more. Add the other egg and mix well. Gradually add the remaining flour mixture, combining well each time.

Sprinkle a little flour on a pastry board and turn the dough out on it. Sprinkle the dough with a little flour, and roll out with a floured rolling pin, sprinkling the dough with a little more flour if it sticks to the rolling pin. Roll the dough out about ¼ inch thick.

With a pizza cutter, pastry wheel, or small sharp knife cut the dough into strips 2 inches wide. Then cut the opposite way into pieces 2½ inches long. With the tines of a dinner fork make rows of fork marks about a quarter of an inch apart on each cookie, like this.

Transfer cookies to baking sheets with a floured pancake turner or spatula. Bake about 12 minutes until cookies begin to brown very slightly on the bottom Remove from oven and baking sheets, and cool on wire rack.

Make frosting for the cookies while they're cooling. Chop the peanuts very finely. Onto a piece of waxed paper sift the confectioners' sugar. Cream the butter in a bowl until soft. Gradually add the sifted confectioners' sugar and mix well. Add the chopped peanuts and the milk and mix well. Spread the frosting evenly on the cooled cookies with a table knife. If frosting doesn't spread easily, add another teaspoon of milk. **Makes 3 dozen.**

Perú

SWEET EGG SQUARES
HUEVOS CHIMBOS

(WAY-vohs CHEEM-bohs)

The literal translation of *Chimbo* is "worn out," "wasted," or like a "bad check." In our country we say a bad check bounces (like rubber) and perhaps *Chimbos* got their curious name from their slightly rubbery texture. In spite of their name, these sweet egg squares are a good-tasting treat. They are best eaten with a fork like a dessert rather than in your hand like a cookie. A recipe almost identical to *Chimbos* is made in Mexico, except that pine nuts are used in place of almonds.

INGREDIENTS:

5 egg yolks
1½ cups water
1½ cups sugar
1 cinnamon stick

2 teaspoons raisins
3 tablespoons slivered
   almonds or other nuts *

UTENSILS: 9-inch by 9-inch baking pan, a large flat baking pan at least 1 inch wider and longer than the 9-inch pan, small bowl, mixing bowl, egg beater, rubber spatula, teakettle, wire rack, small saucepan, measuring cups and spoons, cooking spoons, tongs, table knife, spatula or pancake turner, ruler, low flat dish.

METHOD: Bar cookies (see page 14).

Preheat oven at 350°. Grease the 9-inch by 9-inch baking pan.
Separate 5 eggs. Put the whites in a small bowl and save for another use. Put the yolks in mixing bowl and beat with an egg beater for about 5 minutes, until they are very thick. They should make a slowly dissolving ribbon when you lift

---

* Buy the almonds already sliced or slivered. It is too difficult to slice them yourself.

the beater. With a rubber spatula scrape the yolk into the greased 9-inch baking pan and set it into the larger flat baking pan. Carefully pour some hot (not boiling) water from a teakettle into the larger pan until the water is ½ inch deep. Set the pans in the oven and bake 30 to 35 minutes until the egg yolks become firm. Remove from oven and place the 9-inch pan on a wire rack.

While the egg yolks are baking you can make the syrup. Put the water, sugar, cinnamon stick, and raisins in a saucepan. Bring to boil over medium heat, stirring constantly. Lower heat and simmer 5 minutes without stirring. Remove from heat and lift out the cinnamon stick with tongs.

After removing egg mixture from oven and setting pan on wire rack, cut into 1½-inch squares. Remove the squares from the pan with a spatula or pancake turner. Arrange them on a low flat dish. Sprinkle the almonds over the egg squares. Pour the syrup over all, and allow to cool before eating.

Makes about 3 dozen.

Index

Lithuania, 73

Ma'amoul (Semolina Cookies), 110-111

Maandazi (Fried Cookies), 95-96

Macadamia Nut-Coconut Bars, 136-137

Macaroons
Almond Macaroons, 45-46
Coconut Macaroons, 89-90

Madeleines (Shell-shaped Butter Cakes), 37-38

Makroud el Louse (Almond Cookies in Syrup), 86-88

Manon del Bautismo (Baptismal Cookies), 170-171

Mantecados con Ron (Rum Lard Cookies), 166-167

Maple-sugaring-time Cookies, 148-149

Matanzas Sugar Cookies, 161-162

Màzni Kurabìì (Yogurt-nut Cookies), 64-65

Mazurek Wielkanocny (Easter Cakes), 75-76

Measuring, 22
diameter, 20

Mexico, 159

Methods of cookie-making, 13-16

Miatniye Prianiki (Mint Cookies), 77-78

Mils-sam (Cinnamon Foldovers) 126-127

Mint Cookies, 77-78

Mirrors, 30-31

Missikiti (Coconut Macaroons), 89-90

Mok-si-kyo (Coconut Fritters), 118-119

Molasses
Joe Froggers, 155-156
Molasses Gingersnaps, 56-57

Monterey Jack cheese, 159-160

Muenster cheese, 159-160

Nane Shirini (Persian Cookies), 106-107

Netherlands, 47

Nigeria, 97

Nuts
Brazil Nut Sandwiches, 178-179
Coconut Milk Cookies, 128-129
Flaky Nut Triangles, 100-102
Macadamia Nut-Coconut Bars, 136-137
Maple-sugaring-time Cookies, 148-149
Nut Cakes, 62-63
Nutroll Cookies, 66-68
Sweet Egg Squares, 182-183
Yogurt-nut Cookies, 64-65
See also names of nuts

Oatcakes, 43-44

Orange flower water, 24
Semolina Cookies, 110-111
in syrup and topping for
Almond Cookies, 86-88

Panama, 172

Pancakes, method for making, 15

Panlevi (Sponge Cookies), 163

Pão de Ló (Sponge Cakes), 49-50

Pastillas de Mani (Peanut Squares), 142-143

Peanuts
in frosting, 180-181
Peanut Bars, 99
Peanut Cookies, 97-98
Peanut Squares, 142-143

Pecans, in Holiday Nut Cookies, 79-80

Persian Cookies, 106-107

Peru, 182

Philippines, 142

Phyllo, 13, 100

ABOUT THE AUTHOR

Anita Borghese has been interested in good food and its preparation throughout most of her life. Mrs. Borghese is presently teaching a course in "Down to Earth Cooking" at the Pace University Environmental Center. She and her husband own and run a gourmet health-food shop in Rye, New York, where her specialties include cookies, cakes, and paté. Mrs. Borghese is the author of *The Down to Earth Cookbook* and co-author of *The Complete Book of Indonesian Cooking*. She lives in Pleasantville, New York, with her husband John and her cat Caroline.